CW00496170

A Journey Round the World

Ron Bonney was born in London, and as a child lived through the London Blitz during the second world war. He left school at 14 and worked in the bookselling and publishing industry.

With the advent of computers in the early 1960's he worked on the installation of one of the first computers to be used in commerce and business, and subsequently worked on computer systems design for book publishing companies.

Now semi-retired, he has more time for travelling. He is married with four grown up children and lives in Ruislip Middlesex. This is his first book.

This book is dedicated to Dominic, Georgina, Roseanna, Paula, Heather, and Robert..... my grandchildren.

Travelling the World is always interesting,
                    and on the whole exciting.
It is seldom dull, often shocking,
                    and sometimes frightening.
                                        R.W.B.

A JOURNEY ROUND THE WORLD

Diary of an Overland Trip Across Five Continents

Ronald W. Bonney

DAWSON MILLS
LONDON

A Journey Round the World
First published 1995

Published by
Dawson Mills Publishers
3 Aragon Drive, Ruislip, Middlesex, HA4 9PR. England.

Maps by Claire Bonney and Ron Bonney

The opening lines of the poem 'The Shooting
of Dan McGrew' by Robert W. Service, are
reproduced by kind permission of
M. William Krasilovsky.

ISBN: 0 9526180 0 1

Printed in Great Britain by
The Ipswich Book Company Ltd, Suffolk.

CONTENTS

Acknowledgements

Thanks to my wife Pat for putting up with me being away, and for proof reading when I returned...

Also thanks to the following:

Jill Saxby for proof reading; Claire Bonney for her artistic work and advice on the maps and cover, and especially for teaching me how to do much of it myself; Sarah Bonney for many helpful suggestions; Irene Caple for typing the original diaries as they arrived home every couple of weeks; David Caple for his help and advice on book production and printing; Lars Almgren, travelling friend from Cairo to Kathmandu, for suggesting in the first place that I write the diaries into a book; Ina Teigler, whom I met in Canada, for further encouragement on this idea; John Pert of Yukon Tourism for his interest and help in planning my Alaska and Yukon route; McDonald's Restaurants for their consistently high standards worldwide, especially in a few places where I thought I wasn't going to get a meal that evening, but eventually found a McDonald's.

Introduction

At sixty years old I had the idea to go round the world! Not an organized package tour, but something different! It must be essentially my own thing, something unique! I would travel overland to see as much of the countries as possible, and only travel by air over the seas and oceans.

Having always been an avid reader of travel books, I was painfully aware that I hadn't done anything approaching real travel before. Mind you, I'd seen quite a lot of the world, but mainly on organized holidays! Now I would embark on an adventure planned and carried out by myself.

The idea to do it was one thing, but to galvanize the idea into action was quite another! There were so many questions in my mind about which route to take. How should I travel, and when should I start? I'd have to close my self-employed business and leave my wife and family for however long it would take!

My hobby for the next 18 months was to read travel books and magazines to get some ideas on how I wanted to do it. Eventually I decided I must have some objectives to build into the trip: places I wanted to visit, things I wanted to do in various parts of the world. These objectives ended up by being as follows:

1. Take the traditional overland route going east through Asia to Kathmandu.
2. Visit Alexandria because my late father was in the army and based there during the first world war. He had talked a lot about it and had photographs of his office in the YMCA. I wanted to find a museum of the first world war, and look up the YMCA if it existed!
3. Go to Australia, and also Tasmania, to look up a distant relative descended from a criminal shipped to Tasmania in 1818. My wife was keen to join me on this stage of the

trip.
4. Do some research in the genealogical library of the Mormon Church in Salt Lake City, to further my interest in family history.
5. Travel along the 1,500 miles of the Alaska–Canada highway, which has historical associations with World War 2.

These objectives gave me the key points on a possible route round the world, and in a few months I was able to put together a plan with a starting date 12 months later, which gave me ample time for preparation...total 3 years from idea to starting date!

This diary is a record of the trip I eventually made. It is a journey of 44,000 miles across 5 continents and 21 countries, which took me 31 weeks. Sixteen weeks were spent travelling alone and fifteen weeks with other people. I found that keeping a diary was essential when travelling alone, as it enabled me to share thoughts and travels with family and friends back home, so in fact I wasn't quite so lonely. It also kept them up to date with my journey, as I posted the diary home every two weeks.

Looking back on those weeks spent travelling alone, particularly in America and Canada, I spent a great deal of time poring over bus timetables and maps, in order to check my route and decide what time to depart from places. Also, working out where to stay the night, whether to book ahead or take a chance, and importantly, where to eat! A lot of this time–consuming mundane activity may be reflected in the diary, for which I apologise to the reader...but it was all necessary in order to travel as I did, so I include it. I include also the names of all the hotels, hostels, and other accommodations where I stayed the night...they may be a useful guide to would-be travellers who want budget accommodation. For the record, I stayed the night in 110 different places, not counting numerous nights in buses and trains!

Travelling overland certainly gave me the feel of countries as I passed through them, and I now know a great deal more about the different cultures and religions than I did before. Also, travelling in one continuous journey across the continents of Europe and Asia, and then to Australia, made me aware of, by first hand experience, the gap between the poverty in Asia, and the affluence of the West.

Some years ago the BBC made a television series of Michael Palin travelling round the world in eighty days, following the route taken by a character in a Jules Verne novel. My route crosses Michael Palin's in a few places, and I mention this in my diary. In fact, I was talking to a crew member on the ferry from Italy to Egypt who remembered him travelling with his camera crew!

Many people have travelled round the world in many different ways...some walking, some cycling, others facing extreme hardship and danger in sailing alone round the world. My journey is comparatively ordinary – travelling by train, bus, ferry, and air. Nevertheless, for me, it was a great personal adventure, requiring a great deal of planning, and a certain amount of courage to carry it out.

Some of the places that I visited I was glad to leave, others I would have liked more time to enjoy and explore. Some day I'll return to these places...

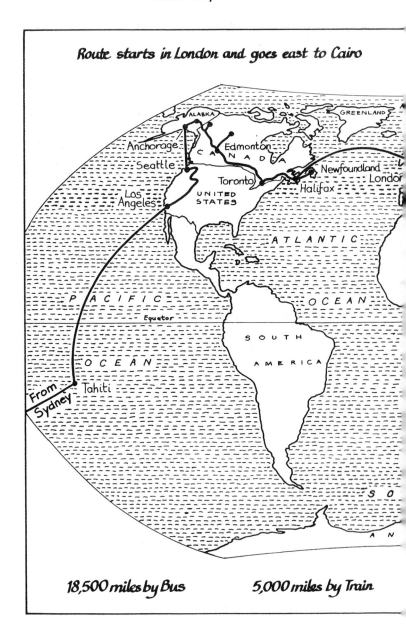

Route starts in London and goes east to Cairo

18,500 miles by Bus   5,000 miles by Train

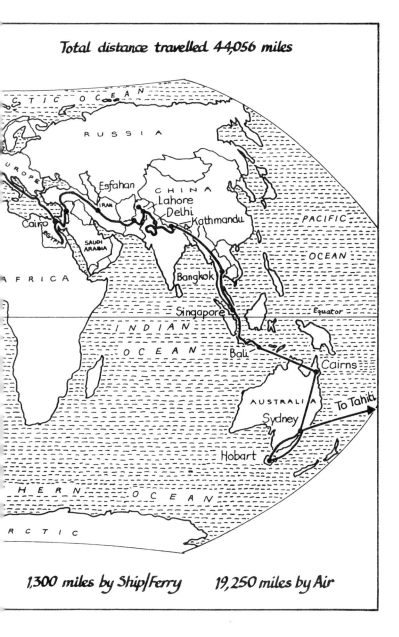

Total distance travelled 44,056 miles

1,300 miles by Ship/Ferry   19,250 miles by Air

5

Stage 1
London to Cairo

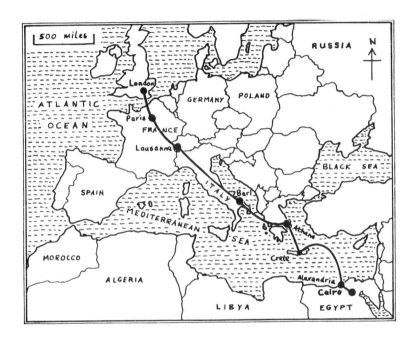

My journey round the world started on the 14th December, 1992, on the 9.15 a.m. train at Victoria Station, London. At Folkestone I caught the ferry to Boulogne, then on to Paris, Lausanne, Milan, and down to the south of Italy to Bari. There I caught the ferry to Alexandria, and train to Cairo, where I joined a Sundowners overland group going to Kathmandu. Distance 2486 miles. The journey took 12 days.

Day 1. Monday Dec 14, 1992. London to Paris.

Here I am on the train, having just left Victoria Station and said good-bye to my wife Pat. What am I doing here..? What have I let myself in for..? I've got 7 months ahead of me travelling round the world, and not the easiest way..!

Nor by the shortest route – I think my route is around 36,000 miles..! I must be crazy..! I could have hopped on a plane to Cairo; stopped over for a few days; then on to Bangkok and Singapore; met Pat for a holiday in Australia; then a stopover at a few other places, and be back home in 5 or 6 weeks..! That would have been nice and comfortable..! Instead, I have to go and make life difficult for myself by giving up Christmas to start with, and then travelling through the Middle East and Asia. My friends must think I'm crazy too, although they actually haven't said..! Then there are all those diseases I could catch; and then a few months ago I went for a medical check up...to make sure I was fit for the journey; what would I have done if the doctor said I wasn't? The doctor said I had high blood pressure, and I must take tablets every day, as well as the many months' supply of malaria tablets...Then there were all the inoculations and vaccinations for Polio, Tetanus, Meningitis, Typhoid, Cholera, Hepatitis and Yellow Fever, enough to give anyone high blood pressure...

The drinks trolley is coming along the corridor of the train...interrupting my train of thought. It's all going to be all right. The three years of planning was the hardest part...now the journey is about to unfold in front of me and all I have to do is sit back and let it happen, and enjoy it...I ordered coffee and sat back and relaxed...

Weather is calm and mild, the train comfortable and uncrowded.

The channel crossing in Catamaran (Sea-Cat) was rough. "Adverse weather conditions," they announced. It was a Swell! I couldn't walk on board at all, and the contents of tables were sliding to the ends, cups as well. It only lasted one hour, not two as in the time table, due to the hour difference. The check-in at Folkestone deposited everyone inside the duty free shop, but I didn't buy anything.

The speed on Sea-Cat was 32 knots, about twice the speed of cruise ships and the normal ferries.

I'm on the Paris train now, uncrowded and on time. Due into Paris Nord 16.36. The changes from train/Sea-Cat/ train, went smoothly, no problems. The taxi to the hotel took a long time to do the 3 kms. as it was the Paris rush hour. Cost 75 fr. but no way was I going by Metro with all my luggage. The Hotel is O.K. Double room with all conveniences. In evening I walked to Gare du Lyon to investigate for the next day's train. Result was: too far to walk, and too difficult by Metro, so it will have to be a taxi again. Ended up in McDonald's for dinner as there were only seedy bars in the area, or posh hotels. Weather O.K. in evening, just a bit cold, but it is December. I'll have to get used to sleeping with my various monies, and airline and ferry tickets in neck wallet, body pouch and waist bag, but there is plenty of room in tonight's double bed! I've forgotten to bring photos of all the family, must phone and ask Pat to send a set to the Cairo hotel.

Night at Hotel des Nations, Paris.

Day 2. Tuesday Dec. 15. Paris to Lausanne.

I'm still getting used to being on my own, it's only when I talk to someone – in English – that I think about my Round the World trip. This is only twice so far. The first was a French lady who was visiting her mother in Paris. She lived in England. I apologized to her for not helping with her luggage when she was obviously having difficulty getting it onto the Boulogne train to Paris. So we talked. I used my head, not my back, as I had a back problem before leaving home. The second was with two young people – not together – waiting for a train at Gare du Lyon. A French girl student, and a Californian fellow on a sort of Round the World trip. He was from San Francisco and the last major place he will visit before returning home will be Iceland, so we had plenty to talk about. Also he had just been to Tromso and Lapland. He wants to go to the Blue Lagoon in Iceland.

Most of the time I'm concerned with the immediate future, i.e. food, money, train. I had a long time to talk to the above people because the Lausanne train was one hour late, although it eventually came in and did depart. But there was much doubt because many trains were cancelled due to a railway strike. A train driver was sentenced to imprisonment a few days ago because he was blamed for a fatal train accident, so the union called a strike. This Lausanne train is a 'super train', called a TGV, and I had to walk a long way along the platform to get to my coach No.18. It has four super locomotives, one at each end and two in the middle, and it's very fast, about 150 mph. It splits in two somewhere, making two trains each with a loco at each end. I hope I'm in the right half!

This morning the lift was out of order, I was on the 4th floor and I didn't want to carry my case down the stairs, the taxi was early and waiting with meter clocking up. Time was critical, although I had planned the timing exactly. Money was the problem! The Bureau de Change was supposed to open at 10.00 but wasn't open by 10.15 so I couldn't wait. The hotel receptionist kindly didn't charge me for breakfast so I could pay the taxi fare. They got the lift working and I finally arrived at the station on time...but as I said, the train was late anyway, also was one hour late arriving in Lausanne.

The Hotel Victoria was only a few hundred yards from the station, an elegant Victorian building, as one would expect, with sweeping curved staircases and pictures of Napoleon at Fontainbleu. Weather is cold, no rain.

Night at Hotel Victoria, Lausanne.

Day 3. Wednesday Dec 16. Lausanne.

This seeems to be all boring detail, but I may as well share thoughts via the paper. Good breakfast, like Swiss ski holiday breakfasts: meats, cheeses and jams, no fruit. I bought bananas. Walked to lake, no sun, but pleasant. I took some photos...I discovered this is a much bigger city than I thought, it rises quite steeply from the lakeside and is very confusing with split levels everywhere. Good dinner last night in a reasonable restaurant, and will go again this evening. Had a drink in the 'Churchill Pub' this afternoon, also took a picture of my train to Milan tomorrow, today, if you follow me, as it runs every day. I know exactly where to stand to get on quickly tomorrow. The Gare du Lyon in Paris and this Lausanne station are both Victorian and not modernized at all, if one can call French and Swiss buildings Victorian.

I think I understand about stations and catching trains, I've done it so often in the last few days! I wonder what delights await me in Alexandria – buying a ticket and getting the train to Cairo. This hotel is like being on a cruise, the room service fellow has changed my towel and tidied up twice already today, it's 7 p.m., but then it's a 4 star hotel. I can't imagine Halifax all that time and distance away...still, one day at a time is all that can happen!

Night at Hotel Victoria, Lausanne.

Day 4. Thursday Dec. 17. Lausanne to Milan.

I had a good meal last night, soup, main course, wine and coffee for £12. Today is sunny. Nice train journey alongside Lake Leman into mountainous area, plenty of snow. "Regardez le Bagage", I hear shouts of this phrase at each stop, so I keep an eye on my case in the rack at end of coach. I have met an American lady with a toddler. She was in the wrong reserved seat. I had an English conversation with her, the first since Gare du Lyon.

I don't like Milan! Went to the Tourist Bureau at the station and they booked me into a 2 star hotel fairly near the station at 45,000 Lira (£22). I didn't want to pay much because I have to leave at 6 a.m. to catch the 7 a.m. train to Bari. Bathroom on the same floor, I didn't care – I didn't want a bath or breakfast! Just outside the Tourist Bureau a policeman approached and asked if I spoke English, asked where my hotel was, and how much? He said it was a bad area, the wrong side of the station, after dark it wasn't safe: peculiar men! He knew a better hotel the other side of the station, the better end, but more money! He said the Tourist Bureau man was getting a commission by sending me there, although it was a hotel in the tourist list of hotels. So who was I to trust? The Tourist Bureau or the policeman? I chose the policeman! So he escorted me to this better hotel opposite the police station, the 'Monopole' where a room with bath cost 107,000 Lira discounted to 70,000 (£34). The staff all spoke English, which figured, as the policeman did too. I wonder how much commission the policeman got? One of the first things I did was to check out the other hotel on the wrong side of the station. It was certainly a seedy area, and I'm glad I changed. My hotel is much nearer the station.

The station...it's enormous...gargantuan! Another Victorian type building. It's more like a cathedral, high domed roofs, statues, statuettes, monolithic pillars, built in massive stone blocks, it looks as if it's just been cleaned. I suppose Milan needs a large station for its teeming masses of people, it's a bit like Hong Kong in this respect. Traffic is heavy too. I haven't gone far from the immediate vicinity of the station in Aeosta Square, which is of similar proportions to the station, and it takes about 15 minutes to walk round it, like walking round the outer edge of Trafalgar Square, only the traffic is worse, if you can imagine it!

I settled for a McDonald's meal this evening, then saw a movie on television in my room and went to bed early. My train arrived here in Milan at 3 p.m. so I've had plenty of time. Alarm set for 5.15 a.m.

Night at The Monopole, Milan.

Day 5. Friday Dec 18. Milan to Bari.

It's 1 p.m., the sun is coming out, and the train has been going alongside the sea since Rimini. It's been misty until now. Train has stopped at Bologna, Rimini, Ancona, Pescara, and passed through Cattolica. It is crowded, the most crowded yet. I got caught in the restaurant car having breakfast when masses of people got on at Bologna. I couldn't get back to my coach to safeguard my seat and luggage, I thought of going along the platform to avoid the people getting on, but decided it was too risky. It took me about half an hour to get back, with so many people waving their tickets and reservations, and finding their seats.

I like Bari, better than Milan anyway. My hotel (Pensione) is comfortable, big twin room with mod–cons, floor is tiled, no carpet. There are palm trees everywhere, much warmer than Milan, Lausanne, Paris. It must be sub–

tropical. The late evening temperature on top of a building was 10°c.

Night at Pensione Giulia di Francesco de Chirico, Bari.

Day 6. Saturday Dec 19. Bari.

This place is teeming with people and cars, and is much bigger than I thought. It's certainly much warmer down here in the south of Italy. Food is cheap, a lot under budget for dinner last night – lasagna, cheesecake, and ½ litre wine for £4.50. I couldn't have less than ½ litre, which is so cheap at 2000 lira, less than £1. You can imagine I was a bit unsteady on my feet after that!

I encountered a problem in my schedule this morning. I went to the port to investigate where the ferry departs from tomorrow, but it's running one day late owing to a seamen's strike last week, and they are unable to catch up the time, so it sails 1700 hrs Monday instead of Sunday. Fortunately I have two nights booked in Alexandria, which will now be only one. Michael Palin was always waiting around for boats which were late! Tried to phone home 3 times this morning, but haven't understood the instructions in Italian. On the first two occasions Pat actually answered.

Night at Pensione Giulia, Bari.

Day 7. Sunday Dec 20. Bari.

Have been to the port this morning and afternoon to check the arrival of my ferry 'Egitto Express'. This morning I managed to understand that it was still in Venice, anchored in harbour due to fog. This afternoon there was no one in the port agent's office. There are other ferries going out to Greece so there are lots of people and vehicles waiting. The port is half an hour's walk away, so I do a lot of walking. I don't trust what they say, so I must go as often as possible. You see, they are not very efficient as a port, the departure board, which is manually operated, still says it is sailing today at 1700 hrs, its scheduled time, they haven't bothered to change it! I met two German men who spoke some English, they are also waiting for the same ferry in their camper van, also a Greek man who turned up to catch the ferry and it wasn't there, he had a problem because he only spoke Greek and Arabic, going to Syria. I shall visit the port once more this evening to see if any ship has arrived, then also first thing in the morning – Monday. I have to leave my case packed in case I have to depart in a hurry. I will also try to post this in the morning. Haven't sent any postcards yet. It's 9.30 p.m. and I have been to the port, but no ship. No information.

Night at Pensione Giulia, Bari.

Day 8. Monday Dec 21. Bari. Egitto Express Sets Sail for Egypt.

It's warm here, daytime temperature is 19°c. I'll be glad to leave Bari, I'm fed up with walking to the port and getting different information each time. The ferry is definitely coming in today. I complained to the tourist office at opening time today (it was shut all the weekend). They phoned the ship's port agent, who said there was someone at the port office yesterday, but I was there morning, afternoon, and evening, for one hour each time, and it was closed (Chiuso) each time. Certainly at normal check-in time of 3 p.m. yesterday, when the ferry should have sailed at 5 p.m., you would think they would have had a representative there to explain to people that the ferry was delayed, and when it was expected. They could have put a notice in their office window, and yet the departure board still said it was sailing at 1700 on 20th December (yesterday). Anyway I checked in at 1.30, boarding at 4 p.m. I am just waiting by the customs in case they change their minds. I can understand Michael Palin waiting around for days, because he travelled on cargo ships not really catering for passengers.

I guess I'm keeping fit, all this walking. I buy lots of bottled water, 1½ litres at a time, and oranges and bananas. I drink the water as I can't keep drinking the local plonk, although it's almost as cheap. The walking and the fresh air and the sunny blue skies all day keep me thirsty. I have pasta dishes for evening meal.

Dodging the traffic in Bari (also Milan) is good exercise too, as one can't very often walk on the pavement, the cars just bump up the pavement and park right up against the shop windows. I've only seen a couple of babies in push chairs, it must be difficult for mothers. Cars just park bumper to bumper, actually touching, and if a driver wants to go, he just gets in his car and sounds the horn continuously, until the driver of the car in front or behind, and so on to the end of the line, moves into some available space, and they all shuffle up a few feet so that someone can get out. The above is made more difficult if you're parked on the pavement and there is a double line of parked cars by the kerb. Many roads have treble parked cars, leaving just about enough room in the middle of the road for moving vehicles and for the pedestrians who are forced to walk in the road. These roads often have only enough width for one car, as most roads are one way streets (Senso Unico). In the above scenario the moving vehicles don't move very fast, fortunately for pedestrians. Buses have to cope with all this somehow. I've often seen buses manoeuvring backwards and forwards in order to turn a corner, because motorists have double parked on all four corners of the crossroad and the bus driver can't turn in one go. The noise is bedlam. As a pedestrian one has to develop a fine sense of timing in order to survive, and if the pedestrian light says 'Go' one has to just step out onto the 'zebra crossing' and walk across, and the cars do actually stop and let you go. The drivers seem to expect you to do this. The motor car has taken over Italy, because I've seen the TV news about the exhaust emissions in Rome, with pictures just like it is here in Bari and Milan. They are getting worried about exhaust fume pollution.

AND THEN ONE SUNDAY AFTERNOON A GREAT SILENCE DESCENDED UPON THE CITY. I walked out of my hotel on Sunday afternoon on my trip to the port, and there was a complete silence and hardly a moving car to be seen, or any pedestrians, so my walk was pleasant. Had they all gone to church? or was there a football match? or was it just siesta time? It didn't happen on Saturday. I never found out why.

It's 7 p.m. and I'm now on board. We set sail on time for Piræus (Athens). The ferry is the 'Egitto Express'. I have a twin cabin for one, and the ship is clean and comfortable. There are not many passengers or vehicles, and everything seems all right. Only important things seem to be announced in English, like lifeboat information etc. Up on deck in the evening it is cool, not uncomfortable in shirt sleeves. The restaurant is self-service, and you can have as much as you can carry on your tray, three meals a day, and pay for wine and water. No coffee at dinner, you have to buy it in the bar, a little cheaper than in Bari, it's 1300 Lira, (1600 in Bari). It's rather pleasant, and a change not having to worry about where I'm going to go for the next meal.

Surprise! surprise! This is what you might call a mini-cruise, we had a Kapitan's Welcome Champagne Party in the lounge. There were nuts, crisps and olives set out nicely. The Kapitan spoke in Italian and German, an interpreter in English and French.

Night on ferry Egitto Express.

Day 9. Tuesday Dec 22. At Sea.

11 a.m. The crew are having their lifeboat drill, passengers have to stay in the lounge. I wish I had my camera with me, one crew member is in the lounge being dressed in his...well, it's like a 'man on the moon suit', aluminium reflective, he's got an axe, ropes, it must be fire fighting drill. The sea is calm, on the starboard is land with mountains in the distance, snow on the tops, we must be in the Ionian Sea. The land could be the Peloponnese Peninsula, because we go through the Corinth Canal later today at 2.30 p.m. heading for Piræus (Athens), where we dock at 6.30 this evening. We put the clocks on one hour last night, total two hours ahead of England. Assuming most people went to the Captain's Cocktail Party, I counted about 100 people, there must be room for a lot more. It's 12 noon and the crew are still having lifeboat drill. They have been at it

for 1½ hours so far. Passengers have to keep out of the way, we can't walk along corridors as all fire doors are closed, luckily I have my notebook with me as I can't get back to my cabin. The interpreter lady has told me that the Commission for Safety at Sea boarded the ship without warning just before sailing from Bari. I saw them studying plans of the ship in the corner of the dining room at breakfast. They are all in suits, collars and ties, walking about with safety manuals asking questions of the crew. Apparently at 10.30 they announced without warning "Safety Drill Now." They announced what passengers must do, as we are not taking part, and they have been at it all this time, although no lifeboats have been lowered. I managed to slip out on deck when no one was looking, and am now forward on top deck, there are a few other passengers here also. The noon-day sun is hot and I obviously cannot stay here for long, because I shall get burnt. It could be mid–summer! Pat and I came through here with friends Rene and Norman Caple in September 1989 I remember, in a ship called 'The Azur', and at the moment the weather is similar. The safety drill has finally ended after 1¾ hours.

7.30 p.m. I took two photos of the Corinth Canal as it is an interesting point in my travels. I expect they will look similar to the ones from the 'Azur'. There was a bit more clearance each side of the ship this time. I've been talking to a bar waiter by the swimming pool, it's not filled in winter, there are 130 passengers and the ship can take 510. He remembers in 1988 when Michael Palin travelled on this ship from Venice to Alexandria, he didn't work on it then, but he heard about it. I have taken a photo of 'Leonid Sobinov' docked alongside us in Piræus.

Logo of Adriatica Navigazione :

I've started drawing to pass the time! It's the shipowner,

and it's on everything, wall and bar decoration, cups, saucers, towels, sheets, ashtrays.

Night on ferry Egitto Express

Day 10. Wednesday Dec 23. Iraklion and at Sea.

11 a.m. Weather is cloudy here and therefore a bit cooler, but still I'm sitting on deck in shirt sleeves. We were allowed ashore from 9 a.m. so I've been for a walk for 1¾ hours. It's an untidy place, although the shops are always clean and tidy inside, but outside there is rubbish everywhere. I took a photo which includes a signpost to Agios Nikolaos – someone has been there, was it my friends Rene and Norman?

2 p.m. Still cloudy and blowy on deck. We have sailed from Iraklion and are now in the Mediterranean. The Ægean Sea stretches from Piræus to Iraklion. I notice that Iraklion is about 35° latitude compared to London which is 52°, so this is a lot nearer the equator. This diary must be a bit monotonous to the reader, but there is not much else to do. A few people boarded the ship at Iraklion, and I've been talking to an American couple from San Diego (she is anyway). He teaches geography at an American school in Sardinia, she works in Italy. They are on holiday and are going to 'drive into the desert' from Alexandria for two weeks.

Night on ferry Egitto Express.

Day 11. Thursday Dec. 24. Christmas Eve. Alexandria.

9 a.m. The ship is just approaching the harbour, it seems peculiar being here on Christmas Eve. I hope everything is all right at home, I'll be thinking of you all over Christmas, and will do my best to phone on Christmas Day. There are two Christmas trees on the ship, and a few other decorations, but there are no particular festivities. It sails for Venice tomorrow. We had to clear out of the cabins early this morning, and have been waiting an hour already and then money–changing into Egyptian Pounds. It was cloudy all day yesterday and is also today, but is not cold.

5 p.m. I have left the familiar world of shipboard life (having been on many cruises), and have been deposited into the noisy chaotic world of Alexandria. Although I only had a few conversations on the ship, there not being many English speaking people, everything was cosy and familiar and comfortable, but now, well...everything is much more unfamiliar than even Bari was. The first thing I did after checking in at the Hotel Semiramis, was to find my way to the railway station. On the way I decided to get away from this place tomorrow, rather than stay two nights as I had intended. The streets and squares are full of rubbish, it's very dusty and there is a wind coming in from the sea, my eyes are smarting from the dust. I went out at 1.30 p.m. and returned at 5.00. The people are shabby, but what could I expect of Egypt having seen Port Said and Cairo? Dodging traffic is also very necessary here, but things could be worse!

I've been to all three tourist offices, and they were all open! At the port on arrival, in the main square where this hotel is, and at the railway station. The staff were all very helpful, but it's the place itself I can't stand. There is no museum containing military exhibits to do with World War 1, which I had hoped to see, as my father was here in 1919. So there is no other reason to stay more than the one night. I may as well move on to Cairo, where at least there may be more tourists than just the one there is here in Alexandria! I said things could be worse, well I was treated with great courtesy at the port, had to show my passport six times to get through immigration, customs, and out of the gate. I was welcomed into the Tourist Police Office, and chatted, and they got me a taxi. Well... they had nothing else to do, there was only me! Not one of the other tourists on the ship was staying in Alexandria, they all had vehicles and were off into the desert, scuba diving, etc. etc.

This hotel is not too bad I suppose, as a 3 star hotel, it's right on the harbour front with a magnificent view of the sea from my 5th floor bedroom. The bedroom is large and grubby, but O.K. I suppose, but I shan't use the bath! It's got dark here between 5 and 6 p.m. My two notebooks are not going to last long at this rate. I shall be glad to meet up with my tour group in Cairo, it's a bit lonely on my own, especially as it's Christmas. The only indication of Christmas is in a few shops and restaurants which have 'Happy Christmas' written on the windows.

I have now to decide where to eat. The tourist office lady recommended a restaurant, but I couldn't find it.

I bought a first class express train ticket to Cairo, and a reserved seat, for 1.55 p.m. tomorrow, Christmas Day. It's a 2½ hour journey. I haven't taken any photos here yet, because when I stop for any reason at all, to look at a map etc. someone comes up to me – "Taxi ride sir?" "Horse and Carriage ride sir?" "To Bombay sir?" – That's some ride! or "You want good disco?"

I had a meal: Fish and Chips. I thought that sounded safe. The waiter kept on saying, "Salad sir, for one?" and I kept on saying, "No salad thank you," remembering about the water it's washed in. But along he came with salad, "Complimentary salad from the Chef!" So what could I do? I didn't eat any, I scooped half of it into a plastic bag which I happened to have on me, then disposed of it later. I apologised for not eating the other half as it was "A bit too much" and "My compliments to the Chef" on his nice fish, chips and salad. Incidentally, there was only me in this large restaurant, but millions of people and cars in the streets, so it was pleasantly quiet. Service was attentive, and it was clean, and cost £4.50 (English) including soup, bread, cola and coffee.

There is a wedding party on the 7th, the top floor of my hotel. I'm on the 5th. The receptionist (proprietor) asked the bellboy to take me up to have a look, it all looked very jolly, but ear piercing noise from the band in the small room.

Night at Semiramis Hotel, Alexandria.

Day 12. Friday Dec 25. Christmas Day. Alexandria to Cairo.

It's been raining here in Alexandria for the last two hours, it will lay the dust. This is the first rain, so far, in the 12 days since I started. I'm sitting in the 1st Class compartment (by Egyptian standards) of the Alex–Cairo Express. Well...I think I am! There are no notices or times displayed in English about trains, only platform numbers. It leaves at 2 p.m. in ½ hour. The information office is closed, as is the tourist office. So I went in to see the Station Master, he saw my ticket and told me clearly "Platform 5" for the Cairo Express, (Turbo Powered, incidentally). At platform 5 a porter grabbed my luggage as I was buying a packaged meat roll, and started up platform 6, having seen my ticket. I argued with him that the Station Master said platform 5, not 6. I must admit the train on platform 6 looked more like an express train than the one on 5. I decided that the porter probably knew better than the Station Master in this shambles of a place! Another passenger confirmed this.

I'm confused about arabic numerals. On the displayed timetables I thought I would recognize train numbers, times, and platform numbers, because they are Arabic, and our English numerals are Arabic, aren't they? But these are not our Arabic numbers! Here they are :

$$1 = 1 \qquad 6 = 7$$
$$2 = ٢ \qquad 7 = ٧$$
$$3 = ٣ \qquad 8 = ٨$$
$$4 = ٤ \qquad 9 = 9$$
$$5 = ٥ \qquad 0 = ٠$$

Both are displayed on the seat numbers. Another passenger was looking at me rather quizzically as I was going down the coach copying down these numbers. He spoke perfect English, and explained that their Arabic language uses Indian numerals and the reason is historical. So now I know! Amazing, we've started dead on time! Why did the English, and other European languages, take the Arabic numerals, while the Arabs changed theirs to the Indian? A mystery! I made a mental note to investigate.

11.15 p.m. The Sundowners group were all here when I arrived at 4.30 p.m. and I have now met them all. Ross, the driver/courier, Joe and Julie, an Australian couple originating from Austria, both about my age, which I knew about from Sundowners in London when I asked what age people were in the group. Lars, a Swedish man about the same age. Then there is Sato, a Japanese man living in Australia, who is deaf, and we have to communicate by writing notes, and making signs. Only five passengers and two couriers, the other courier is called Carol, and we meet her in Aqaba, where she has the 32 seater Mercedes coach doing another trip which she finishes in 10 days time. We don't need a coach for these first 10 days, as we go to Aswan and Luxor by train, then back to Cairo by train, then get a taxi and ferry to Aqaba. This is all inclusive in the cost. In the middle of Turkey, Göreme on the itinerary, we meet up with another driver who will have just driven a new 25 seater bus from London. We swap coaches and the bigger one is driven quickly to Kathmandu without passengers, where it is needed for another trip. Officially this trip doesn't start until 6 p.m. 26th December, tomorrow, but in fact we are meeting tomorrow after breakfast.

I was suffering from culture shock in Alexandria (where I phoned Pat), and was very homesick. In the first place, I was on my own; secondly, I had just arrived in Egypt which was very different from Europe; thirdly, it was Christmas. Now there is company! It's still Christmas Day... 11.58 p.m.

Night at Fontana Hotel, Cairo.

Stage 2
Cairo to Kathmandu

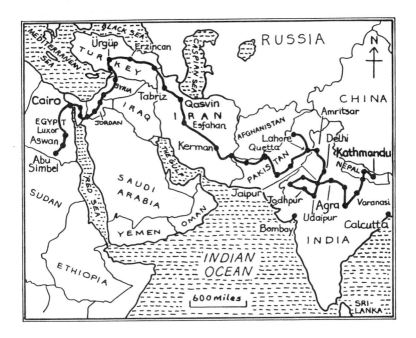

This was an 8 week overland trip by coach organized by Sundowners, a part of the Encounter Overland Group. There were 5 passengers, a courier, and driver. We actually travelled by taxi and train for the first ten days in Egypt, then caught the ferry to cross the Gulf of Aqaba, and picked up the coach in Aqaba, Jordan. Distance 9,600 miles, 58 days.

Day 13. Saturday Dec 26. Boxing Day. Cairo.

It's warm! 3 p.m. I don't get much time to write this diary, it seems. This morning it took 4 hours to find a bank that changes travellers' cheques, and Joe was supposed to know where to go because he and Julie have been here 10 days already. I had to change money for myself and for the group's 'bed and board' fund which provides accommodation and two meals a day as from the meal this evening. Ross, our leader, has very kindly brought a Christmas cake and bottle of whisky from England which we are apparently going to consume this evening after the evening meal. We have changed rooms this morning as the trip is based on two people sharing twin rooms. I am with Sato, the Japanese/Australian who is deaf, but during the trip we change around a bit. At 3.45 p.m. we are going on an optional excursion to a Son et Lumiere show at the Pyramids. It starts at 6.30 and we are going by Metro and mini-bus. The Metro is the only civilized place I have seen in this shambles of a city, and it only costs 25 piastres (5p).

I was encouraged to try a little local food last night, it was like two hamburgers, only it was really Kebab with onion etc. Total cost was 80p. It tasted good and I still feel O.K. As I was still hungry I went back to my room and had a cheese roll (from the buffet on the train) and orange and mandarin I still had from the ship.

I'm getting a bit behind with diary...

To the keen student of 'art nouveau' it might be thought that there is a new art form in the many differing shapes and sizes and contents of the piles of rubbish in the streets, and an even better appreciation might be had from the 10th floor cafe in our hotel, of each and every rooftop in the city. They don't go to the 'dump', they throw it in the street or take it up to the roof! Actually, on closer inspection, the rubbish is all paper, cardboard and builders' rubble. It isn't particularly unhygienic. If they re-deployed all the street shoe shine boys into rubbish clearing jobs, the streets wouldn't be so dusty.

Today I walked with Joe and Julie (Australian couple) and Lars (Swedish) to find a bank to change money, and later met our courier at the Hilton hotel at 4 p.m. to set off for the light and sound show at the Pyramids. The Hilton, of course, was clean and of typical English standard. We used the Metro to get to the Hilton – 3 stops – you can go 7 stops for 5p (English) or 10p if further. The light and sound show was like the one at the Acropolis in Athens, but better really, it was done as if the Sphinx was the narrator, telling the story of ancient Egypt with the various temples or pyramids (3) lit up at the appropriate time. We arrived just after sunset when the sky was all red, and on the horizon between two pyramids were 3 camels and riders, like three wise men (so someone said). I haven't seen or felt a mosquito yet!

Night at Fontana Hotel, Cairo.

Day 14. Sunday Dec 27. Cairo.

I realized I have repeated things a bit yesterday, getting a bit mixed up when I don't keep up to date. Today we hired a taxi for 6 people and visited the Citadel, which I didn't go in because I went in 1989, and the City of the Dead, which we saw in 1989, but we went in this time and saw a lot of people living in tombs of about 200 years old. The tombs they built even only 200 years ago were well built brick rooms, and are better accommodation now than ordinary shanty towns in most cities today. The people are just squatters, they have television in some of them. The place was clean and tidy compared to the city. Our taxi driver/guide invited us into the tomb of his parents, which he keeps locked! Some of his friends came in also, and incantations were made.

With great trepidation I joined our group at a wayside cafe for a cup of tea. It was on a corner of a crossroads inside this huge cemetery. There were rickety benches and tables. I drank most of my tea, with sugar, no milk with tea here. I have had some fresh carrot and fruit juice in the town, they make it while you watch, they feed the peeled carrots into a liquidiser until there is half a glass of juice, then they cut fresh oranges and put them into a squeezer until the glass is full up. One glass costs 20p English. You can have other combinations of fruit. I toured bazaars before going back to hotel.

Night at Fontana Hotel, Cairo.

Day 15. Monday Dec 28. Cairo.

Today we went to Memphis, one of the old capitals of Egypt, then to Saqqara, which is the necropolis (burial place) for the city of Memphis, it stretches some 30 km along the Nile, although we only visited the northern tombs. We again went to the Pyramids in the afternoon so the others could do the guided tour. I didn't do it as I had previously experienced it in 1989. We boarded our train at 8 p.m. for the overnight trip to Aswan. It was a 1st Class Sleeper and quite good, with beds made up at night, and airline type meals, dinner and breakfast.

Overnight on Sleeper Train to Aswan.

Day 16. Tuesday Dec 29. Aswan.

Arrived Aswan 12 noon. Incidentally, we are all learning some sign language, as it avoids having to write everything down to communicate with Sato, our Japanese–Australian fellow passenger. Everywhere we go he manages to find a local deaf person and they meet and they have a chat together, there being no language difficulties for them. This afternoon we hired a Felucca (Sail Boat) although there was no wind and the boatman had to row. He was 'out of his depth' when he got stuck on a sandbank, and had to be rescued by a passing Felucca with an engine. The boatman took us to a friend's house in a Nubian village, for a cup of tea. His house was made of proper brick, but most of the others were mud brick huts. The sights and sounds of all these places is overwhelming, as it is also with my friend Lars. I must take it easy and not do too much, but it is difficult at the moment not to go on the excursions, our guide tries to get us to go on so many trips, but he is young. Sometimes we all resist a second trip in one day.

Night at Hather Hotel, Aswan.

Day 17. Wednesday Dec 30. Aswan.

It is much warmer here in Aswan. Today we got up at 3.30 a.m. to depart on a mini-bus trip to Abu Simbel, 280 kilometres south of Aswan, and not far from the Sudan border. It's a much used tourist route. The idea was to visit the place in the morning while still cool and be back by about 2 o'clock. It took 3½ hours each way. Abu Simbel is a very important place, both for Egyptology and for modern times. It was necessary for Egypt's future to build the Aswan Dam in order to control the flood seasons of the Nile, and also create a reservoir, Lake Nasser, which is 500 kilometres long. Unfortunately the two temples of Ramses II, which are 3200 years old, would be in the way of the new reservoir, and must somehow be saved at all costs. This was done in the 1960's by an international UNESCO team, which took 4 years and 4 million $US to achieve. The temples and colossal statues 33 metres high were carved out of the solid rock in-situ by the ancient Egyptians, so it was a formidable task to move it all up the mountain 210 metres away and 65 metres higher, and still retain an orientation with the sun's rays on a particular point inside the temple two days each year: February 21st, the king's birthday, and October 22nd the date of his coronation. The task is reckoned by Egyptologists to at least have paralleled the skill of the ancient artisans who chiselled the temples out of the cliff face 3200 years ago. You can imagine that the idea of this momentous task grips my imagination, and I feel I want to research it a bit more to understand it completely.

Night at Hather Hotel, Aswan.

Day 18. Thursday Dec 31. Aswan to Luxor.

Today we travelled by taxi from Aswan to Luxor, stopping for coffee and for visiting Kom Ombo Temple by the Nile. The taxis we use are large Peugeot 504 Estate cars with three rows of seats and it gets a bit hot in a taxi with 6 people and a driver. We visited Luxor Temple when we arrived.

In the evening at the hotel, we had a special New Year's Eve buffet plus a show until midnight. It was an Egyptian belly dancer, which we all got fed up with and left at 11.15, the Egyptian music was terrible.

Night at Windsor Hotel, Luxor.

Day 19. Friday Jan 1. New Year's Day. Luxor.

Up early again today to leave at 5.45 a.m. to visit the
Valley of the Kings before the sun gets too hot. The tombs
are incredible and magnificent palaces hewn out of the rock.
No photographs were allowed. This evening we will see the
Sound and Light show at Karnak Temple, then go round it
in the daylight tomorrow, then catch the 8 p.m. overnight
sleeper train back to Cairo. My daily output of writing
seems to be getting much less, although I have written
many postcards.

Night at Windsor Hotel, Luxor.

Day 20. Saturday Jan 2. Luxor.

The Sound and Light show last night was all right, except
there were too many people at the English show, about
1000. It's amazing the number of tourists here. Have been
round Karnak Temple today, it was very good and we had a
good guide and she didn't mind all the questions I had to
ask.

We are now on the Night Sleeper Train to Cairo, and
have just had dinner which wasn't very hot, but enjoyable as
it was international airline type food, and I haven't liked the
Egyptian food very much.

Overnight on Sleeper Train to Cairo.

Day 21. Sunday Jan 3. Cairo to St. Katherines.

Today we start our overland trip in earnest as our trip
south to Aswan and Luxor was merely diversionary activity,
but nevertheless it was wonderful to see all the temples and
tombs of the ancient Egyptians.

Today was a disaster from beginning to end! Woken at
6 a.m. on the train for breakfast which was supposed to be
one hour before arrival in Cairo at 7 a.m. but it arrived at
10 a.m. We had hired a taxi for the two day trip to
Nuweiba, where we catch the Aqaba ferry. The taxi was
arranged in advance by Ross, our courier. We didn't know
if it was going to meet us at Cairo Station or the Fontana

Hotel. You are never sure of any arrangements made with, or the answers to questions from, Egyptian people. I had to go to the Fontana Hotel to ask about mail, and Ross came with me while the others waited at the station with the luggage. (Pat's letter hasn't arrived – they will forward it to the hotel at Kathmandu). We saw the taxi driver and told him to take the taxi over to the station while we walked across. One hour later..! we got fed up with waiting, so Ross went back to the hotel...The taxi driver was still waiting for us there! The next hour was taken up with us complaining that the roof rack was not any good for luggage. (It was like the ones you use for skis, windsurf boards etc.) Eventually he swapped it with the roof rack of one of his friends. All the Egyptian taxi drivers argued together about the problem, then they'd break off and tell us there was 'no problem'.They argue like the Italians! They insisted for ages that the 'windsurf roof bars' were no problem for lots of luggage. When they finally agreed to make the change, it was still 'no problem'. We finally set off for the Iranian embassy because two of our party did not have Iran visas. This took another hour until 1 p.m. We stopped for coffee at a roadside cafe, and 20 kilometres after leaving Joe suddenly remembered he'd left his bag there containing all his money and video camera! What a find that would have been for someone! We got it back but lost 40 minutes. It was 420 kilometres from Cairo to our overnight stop at St.Katherines, and we still had a long way to go.

We went through Suez and under the Suez Canal, travelling south down the east side of the canal, as I did in 1989, only then it was the west side. We could see the ships in the canal all the way. Then we travelled alongside the Gulf of Suez for some way before turning east to get to St. Katherines, our night stop. This was not booked. The road was all tarmac except for one ½ mile stretch. It was 4.30 and just beginning to get dark, we were right in the middle of the Sinai Desert, when during this ½ mile stretch of gravel, we got a puncture. The car 'jack' wasn't much good and wouldn't lift the wheel off the ground, so four men (not me) took it in shifts of two to hold the car up while the wheel was changed. Eventually, a passing army truck stopped and two kind soldiers, seeing our plight, stopped to help and finally took over the job themselves with their own 'jack', while our taxi driver and his brother stood back and let them get on with it without any supervision! A few miles into the desert we learnt that the soldiers must have looked good, but 'didn't have a clue', because the peculiar jolting noise coming from the rear was the wheel loose! There were two bolts with stripped thread! They had taken the jack away before the nuts were tight enough, therefore the wheel wasn't aligned properly when the nuts were tightened. We limped along a few miles at a time and stopped, all got out, unloaded luggage, jacked up the car as high as it would go, tightened the nuts as much as possible, and carried on for another few miles until the clonking of the loose wheel got too bad... and so on.

The car was overloaded with 8 people and luggage for 6. Progress was slow... and it was dark now. The taxi driver had brought his brother because it was a two day journey finishing at Nuweiba, on the Gulf of Aqaba, and maybe because of the hazardous nature of the journey, but the two of them didn't seem to know what they were doing most of the time and each time we limped a shorter distance than the time before. The jack never lifted the wheel off the ground, and each time the nuts got worse and the bolts started bending where they fit on the wheel. We finally halted when it would have been folly to have carried on with the wheel so loose. It clonked at each turn! So there we were in the middle of the Sinai Desert, a lovely moon shining, everyone was getting cold and we dare not say much to the taxi drivers, as they were in a bad mood, and would start arguing. Julie had a cold and was shivering, we were expecting to spend the night in the desert, using our emergency sleeping bags. There wasn't any traffic, but finally a car did come and it stopped, and one taxi driver got a lift to St. Katherines, now 20 kilometres away. 40 minutes later he came back in a taxi, another Peugeot 504 with a roof rack. We slowly escorted the limping taxi a few kilometres to the next road block/check point (there are many of these, manned by soldiers with automatic rifles) where we left it, and carried on to St. Katherines, now with 9 people aboard and crammed with luggage.

Overloading vehicles is the thing they do here in Egypt. The local buses have people hanging on the back and sides, and we have seen children getting a lift by standing on the coupling between railway carriages, I presume they get off at a station when no one is looking! We arrived at St. Katherines at 11.30 p.m. Its only a small village with a tourist hotel of sorts, and wonder of wonders, they found us accommodation, although very basic, and laid on a meal with hot soup and coffee. We got to bed at 1 a.m. the beds being thin mattresses on concrete beds. It was very cold, so we had to use our sleeping bags.

Night at Al Fairoz Hotel, St. Katherines.

Day 22. Monday Jan 4. St.Katherines to Nuweiba.

St. Katherine's Monastery is half way up Mount Sinai, where, on the summit, Moses had proclaimed to him by God, the ten commandments. That's why this village has a hotel, for the constant stream of visitors going to the summit of Mount Sinai. We hadn't time to do this, but we visited the monastery. It is what you might call a 'live' Monastery with Monks. One was talking to visitors in the chapel. Sinai is a barren land, mainly desert and low mountains, a few Bedouin tribes and camels scattered about. We passed a few oil installations on the coast, but there's nothing much else here.

We started off again today with a different taxi, a Mercedes saloon, but we managed to all get in plus luggage. We headed out across the desert for Nuweiba, 110 kilometres away. This is on the Gulf of Aqaba and is a seaside village and port, where we catch the ferry to Aqaba. The only place we could stay was in holiday chalets. They were set in a very nice beach area, with palm trees on the beach, but it's all a bit shabby. The weather is warm and the sea looks pleasant.

Night at Holiday Chalets, Nuweiba.

Day 23. Tuesday Jan 5. Nuweiba to Aqaba.

We took a taxi to the port to catch the 11.30 ferry. It was very shabby, although we went tourist class (the highest). The other class, used by the locals, we never saw, as we were completely segregated. Arrived Aqaba at 3 p.m. and met by our proper courier named Carol, with a 30 seater coach. We are in a nice hotel for one night, and move on to Petra tomorrow.

Jordan is different! Well... it could be England in some areas. It's much cleaner than Egypt and we haven't had anyone touting for business, or 'Bak-sheesh'. There are pictures of King Hussein everywhere in shops, hotels, offices, the port, and on car stickers. From Nuweiba, and also from the ferry, we saw the mountains of Saudi Arabia on the other side of the Gulf.

Night at Hotel Alcazar, Aqaba.

Day 24. Wednesday Jan 6. Aqaba to Petra.

On our way to Petra we visited Wadi Rum of Lawrence of Arabia fame in 1918. The valley is a geological wonder, with 1400 ft. cliffs rising from both sides of the valley. This is in the middle of the desert although there is a village here for tourists. We arrived at Petra at 6 p.m. and found a hotel. Our courier and driver have to take it in turns to sleep in the coach to guard against anyone breaking in!

Night at Flowers Hotel, Petra.

Day 25-26. Thursday-Friday Jan 7-8. Petra to Damascus.

We stayed in Petra last night in a new hotel, Flowers Hotel, just one week old... very nice! Spent this morning walking round the Petra sights, it was alright but did not compare with Egypt's.

11 a.m. Friday. We are waiting in 'no man's land' between the Jordan and Syria border, having just spent our Jordanian dinars and changed some money into Syrian pounds. We left Amman at 7.45 this morning heading for

Syria. We have hardly seen Amman, as we arrived at hotel 7.45 last night in the dark and pouring rain (the first since Alexandria). On these one night stops we don't see much unless we arrive in the afternoon, then there is time to explore a bit before dinner. We have eight 'one night' stops in a row after Cairo. Getting up early is difficult, sometimes not having time to do all necessities before leaving after breakfast. I'm coping with the rigours of overland travel, and now we have the coach I'm not taking my case off the coach at night stops, just packing an overnight bag.

Carrying my luggage around has been a bit of a problem as my trolley doesn't go up or down steps, or over rough ground, but Lars, my Swedish friend, often carries my luggage up steps. Anyway, I'm fit apart from a cold, which was inevitable as we are always together. Out of our original six people I was the 5th to catch a cold! We have two extra people with us from Amman to Göreme (Turkey) who were on the previous Middle East trip with this bus. They are both Australian – brothers, who will make their own way from Göreme to Cairo via Ephesus, Crete and Alexandria.

2 p.m. and getting cold. Now it's 3.0 p.m. and snowing, just approaching Damascus. Heavy snow! After checking in to the hotel, Lars and I went on what turned out to be a 'wild goose chase'. I was trying to locate the address I had of a Radio Amateur in Damascus, but we never found it!

I like Syria, although politically it doesn't like the Brits. We appear to be bottom of the league table of visa entry fees they charge to foreigners. Of our international group from five countries, it ranges from nothing at all for Australians, to £37.50 for British people. What's more, we've only just been promoted to be on the league table at all! Two years ago we weren't allowed in. However, all the Syrians, the border guards, customs, immigration officials, hotel staff and waiters, all present an image of 'Welcome to our Country' and are extremely pleasant and polite.

Our dinner in Damascus was a culinary delight of oriental food. Our couriers had booked a table for 9 at this restaurant near the hotel. They had inspected the menu and decided it was a 'cheapie' suitable for our budget, which we had been over-spending in Egypt. The restaurant looked respectable... we were shown upstairs into a palatial dining room and were treated like royalty. The manager said he had something special for us. "Have soup first," there was a choice of three. Bottled water came, and pitta bread (much better than the Egyptian variety). Hors d'oeuvre came next which was really many plates of salad, cheese, pasty rolls, meat rolls, dips, pickled vegetables, spring onions and plates of English type chips. The dips were spicy, but not garlic, and of course olives, one gets olives for breakfast and all meals.

We did not know that all this was just for starters, although we did wonder! In the middle of all this we were presented with large pieces of pitta bread about 18 inches in diameter and freshly baked. While recovering from this starter the proprietor came in with his notebook and another waiter, as interpreter, and wanted orders for 'dinner'. We all looked down at our expanding waist lines in dismay! What could we do? We ordered small ones. I had kebab, but it wasn't small with all the trimmings. It ended with Turkish coffee. Everything was presented as you would expect in an expensive restaurant. We were worried about the extent our budget would go over the top, but it came to the princely sum of £2.45 each person (English) including tip. I will have to buy a car sticker I LIKE SYRIA.

Nights at Cameo Hotel, Amman.
Imad Hotel, Damascus.

Day 27. Saturday Jan 9. Damascus to Aleppo.

Spent the morning in Damascus, the oldest continuously inhabited city in the world. We looked round the Azem Palace and its museums, also went round one of the many covered bazaars in the old city, called 'souqs'. It's very cold here, near freezing point with snow on the hills outside town. I searched hard and managed to find a box of tissues in the souq for my cold! We left about noon for Aleppo. Arrived late, about 6.30 p.m. so didn't see much of the town and we had dinner in our hotel. The Hotel Baron is where Lawrence of Arabia stayed, also Agatha Christie and

Lady Mountbatten. It was obviously a very grand hotel in those days, but is now a bit shabby and run down, and therefore not too expensive for our budget.

Night at Hotel Baron, Aleppo.

Day 28. Sunday Jan 10. Aleppo to Adana.

Left Aleppo at 8 a.m. for Turkey. It took 2½ hours to get through the border, which apparently is quite good for this crossing. We would have been a lot quicker if the customs man at the Turkish side hadn't insisted on learning how to play English patience with the cards that a member of our group had left out on the table in the coach, instead of helping his colleague look for all the contraband we might have been carrying, but I guess he held the trump card!

Turkey is green and cultivated compared with the endless deserts we've been crossing in Egypt, Jordan, and Syria. Money is 13000 lira to the £, worse than Italy. Money is a big problem, you mustn't change too much when you enter a country, otherwise you don't spend it all and therefore suffer a severe loss when you exchange it for the new currency at the border. You get used to Egyptian pounds, then it's Jordanian dinars, then Syrian pounds, now Turkish lira. I have to watch these money changers like hawks. They always round down to the next lowest convenient amount if you don't question it, or just give you a bundle of notes which they hope you won't count! You must ask what the exchange rate is, otherwise you have no hope of checking it. They won't change travellers' cheques and therefore don't give a receipt. One of our group nearly got caught for £10 short in his exchange, if I hadn't brought it to his notice. Drink is cheap here. Lars gives me a little Vodka in the evening, the local one costs only $2 (American) for a 75cl bottle. We have strict instructions to consume all alcohol before entering Iran, as it would be unthinkable to take any there!

Every border crossing is a hazard if you have a video camcorder! Joe has one, and it causes a major incident each time we enter a country; all the customs men come out of their office and board the coach to inspect this piece of equipment, turn it over, hold it up to the light, open it up, inspect the batteries, register it in a book, stick a number on it. In some places he has to fill in a declaration form and show a receipt. He was not allowed to use it at many historic monuments in Egypt unless he paid an enormous fee. I'm glad I didn't get one!

Night at Duyug Hotel, Adana.

Day 29-31. Monday-Wednesday Jan 11-13. Ürgüp.

The Adana stop was instead of Iskenderun in the itinerary, also Ürgüp instead of Göreme, although this is still the Göreme valley. I haven't written much these last few days as I haven't been well, missed the whole day excursion Tuesday, stayed in bed the whole morning. Not like me! When we arrived here, the hotel appeared to be closed, they opened up just for us. It was freezing cold, and the central heating wasn't working properly – they had an engineer in to fix it, but it only got going properly on Wednesday night.

Ürgüp is like a ski village without skiers – roads, hills, mountains, all deep in snow. I have bought leggings to wear under trousers for when it gets really cold! The night air temperature here is only -19°c (minus) and looking at the T.V. weather map it is colder in eastern Turkey and northern Iran, which is our route for the next few days. Is this making you shiver? For all I know it could be as cold in England as I haven't heard any news since Amman. However, this place has its compensations, for if you feel cold when in the village, you just stop and look in a shop window, and the proprietor immediately comes rushing out, inviting you in to warm in front of a gas boiler fire, which all shops have and you are given hot Turkish tea without any pressure to buy anything, although my friend Lars did buy a Turkish carpet at enormous expense. Some of the group had a Turkish bath on Tuesday evening, but I decided it would be foolish for me to, as I had a bad cold.

3 Nights at Panorama Hotel, Ürgüp.

Day 32. Thursday Jan 14. Ürgüp to Erzincan.

We left Ürgüp at 7 this morning as we have 520 kilometres to go to Erzincan and didn't know what road conditions would be like as we go further east and higher through the mountains. So far, 11 a.m. all roads are clear of snow, there hasn't been any fresh snow for some days.

We have just stopped for a tea break at a roadside café, where some man, who was very interested in us as a group and in our route on the map, bought us all tea. The place was full of men smoking and playing dominoes and whist. You don't see any women in these places, in fact, you don't see many anywhere. It seems that in these countries they are kept out of sight! You can imagine that when we turn up at a café in our tour bus with our tour leader at the wheel, who is a petite young woman, we cause a minor sensation with all these men. She usually walks in at the head of the group, nonchalantly, and casually sorts out what the menu is in English, organizes who wants tea or coffee, where is the loo? etc. The sounds at the game tables suddenly cease, all heads turn as one, to gaze at this sight! Eventually most go back to their games, but those who have nothing better to do except sit round the fire will continue to stare in amazement, until we leave. She is unperturbed!

The people are kind and good to us – one man delved into his bag and presented us all with a huge orange each, which the proprietor peeled and sliced. It went down well with our breakfast of scrambled egg.

12 noon. Hills and plains are all covered in snow; it's a sunny, cloudless sky, but very little snow melts in the sun.

Night at Galliston Hotel, Erzincan.

Day 33-35. Friday-Sunday Jan 15-17. Erzincan to Qasvin.

I haven't written anything for the past 3 days as I have a 'sick bowel'. It didn't seem to get any colder during these three days – just very cold! I have been eating alright, but not too much of anything, and drinking as much as possible.

12 noon – Iran. This is just the same as N.E. Turkey – snow, ice, mountains, plains. Iran I think of as Persia, and of desert lands – maybe it is, but we can't see it for snow, and the rivers are just a trickle through the ice floes. We are stuck on a mountain pass because of an accident a few hundred metres ahead. A bus has gone over the side into a river alongside the road and there is heavy lifting equipment pulling it out. The river seems to be frozen.

Travelling is hard when you are not feeling well, 10 hours a day, 15 hours yesterday as we were 6 hours getting across the border, stops for tea and lunch, find a hotel, leave early in the morning and sometimes stop for breakfast if it is too early for breakfast in the hotel. Breakfast is the best meal as we always get eggs, scrambled or fried. Other meals everyone gets fed up with – kebab or chicken. In Turkey they did at least give you a gravy or sauce with the meat and rice, but here in Iran you just get plain meat covered in rice which is bland and tasteless. We do get soup though, which is good. It would be interesting to see an Iranian cookery book...the smallest one in the world!

This place is like what I thought Siberia was like, although I've never been there. Thousands of miles of snow covered land. I'm wrong! Carol, our courier, has been on the Trans–Siberian Express and says it has many forests and is much more interesting than this!

Our one week's continuous travel through this harsh countryside is fraught with hazard as evidenced by the coach crashing into the river this morning, but the coaches could break down, have punctures etc. I have mentioned before that we were to meet up with a second Sundowners' coach and driver at Ürgüp, central Turkey. The driver had come direct from London with a newly re-furbished coach and many spare parts, axles etc. which is to be delivered to the Kathmandu office. We have now learned that this rendezvous was planned with the hazardous nature of our journey through this frozen waste in mind. It is better with two coaches and three drivers if anything goes wrong! We are fortunate that Andy, the driver of the new coach, is a qualified Heavy Goods Vehicle mechanic. He's Australian from Perth. So far we've had one puncture on the new coach, and on the old coach a brake valve sometimes seizes up over-night with the cold and has to be thawed out with a primus stove. The two coaches travel together and if one gets too far behind, the other waits for it to catch up. The passengers can travel in either coach. I like the big old one better as I can walk about, and it has a seat with a table where I can write.

Nights at Hotel Isfahan, Dogubeyazit.
Hotel Darya, Tabriz.
A Hotel in Qasvin.

Day 36. Monday Jan 18. Qasvin to Esfahan.

Today we bypass Teheran heading for Esfahan. It is just a little less cold today. The landscape reminds me of pictures of the moon, because more snow melts in the sun each day and all the surfaces are smoothed over, and everywhere glistens, giving an eerie effect. I sometimes wonder why I'm taking malaria tablets as there surely can't be a live mosquito within a thousand miles of this place. I suppose it's possible they contribute to my sick bowel, but still I take them!

Night at Hotel Asfahan, Esfahan.

Day 37. Tuesday Jan 19. Esfahan.

Night at Hotel Asfahan, Esfahan.

Day 38. Wednesday Jan 20. Esfahan to Kerman.

Esfahan is the city of 'A Thousand and One Nights', although I never saw any evidence of it. We had a conducted walking tour of the city in the morning, looking at the beautiful mosques and many bazaars, also unusual bridges over the river. Temperature is just a few degrees below freezing, so quite pleasant, comparatively, for walking, also the sun shines from morning until night. They only have 136 mm. of rain per year – I don't think I'd like it in the summer!

In the afternoon in Esfahan we set out to the bazaars again and I really intended to buy some gifts. I have not bought anything so far except food and drink, whereas the others have bought many things. However I never got to the bazaar, I had to leave the others and find the nearest loo which happened to be in a mosque, then went back to the hotel, not wishing to have any more unpleasant experiences. I have, of necessity, come to work out how to use the loos in this part of he world, without seats or paper! When one has diarrhoea, one has no choice! In the evening we had a slap up proper meal in another hotel restaurant. Well, for me not quite so 'slap up' as I had to be a bit careful. We decided to have a nice meal when we heard about this restaurant as we had been living on kebabs and rice for longer than we cared to remember, and our 'bed and board' kitty was getting quite rich, so we decided to splash out. I had grilled trout, which was excellent.

Today, Wednesday, we set off from Esfahan at the early hour of 6.30 a.m. as it is 703 km. to Kerman, tonight's stop. It was snowing so there were a few inches of snow on the roads, being too early for the grit lorries. It was slow going for the first two hours until the snow had been pounded by the traffic. Now, in the early afternoon, we have travelled further south and the roads are clear of snow, we can actually see the desert with only a few patches of snow. So it seems that our journey through the frozen wastes to the north has ended! A guide book that we have on the coach says that only those with masochistic tendencies will attempt to travel the route we have taken in winter. We now look forward to the warmer climate ahead. It's a long way to Bali!

Night at Hotel Akhavaan, Kerman.

Day 39. Thursday Jan 21. Kerman to Zahedan.

This note was on our hotel bedroom door:

In the name of God, Khavar Hotel says wel come
to you dear guest.
IMPORTUNT TELEPHONE NOMBERS: RECEPTION

AND IN FOR MATION   102
RESTURUNT   104
BUGAGE TRANSPORT   102

Interesting spelling and spacing! This is the last stop before the Pakistan border. It's been so hot this afternoon we all sat outside a roadside bar for lunch in shirt sleeves. We have certainly left the snow behind now – haven't seen any since before the last mountain range this morning. It's just desert and scrub land...uninteresting!

Night at Khawar Hotel, Zahedan.

Day 40. Friday Jan 22. Zahedan to Dalbandin.

Arid desert and mountains in the distance – we are now in Pakistan and have filled up with diesel fuel, at a desert filling station...well, a shed with barrels of fuel all over the sand, and you fill up a 5 litre can by means of a tap and carry it over to the bus...and so on until you have enough. It was rather pleasant to see little boys playing cricket by the roadside –   reminds me of home!

We are now at Dalbandin for our night stop and it is the most basic accommodation yet, and I hope, for the trip. It is, apparently, similar to the accommodation at Nok Kundi, which was our scheduled night stop, just bare rooms with concrete floors, stone walls, bedsteads, some with mattress, some without, and a toilet of sorts. We have to use sleeping bags here as there are no bed covers. All five of us slept in two rooms with inter-communicating doors. It was very cold!

Night at Dak Bungalow, Dalbandin.

Day 41. Saturday Jan 23. Dalbandin to Quetta.

We were called early by Carol to say we were having breakfast on the roadside by the coach. The larger coach had spare supplies of baked beans and coffee and someone had bought bread yesterday. We had butter from Turkey which had satisfactorily been kept cold by merely being in the coach. There was also a primus stove for heating. The early morning was bitter cold – Lars and I kept warm while waiting for breakfast by cleaning and wiping the inside of the coach, which was very dirty from the very dusty ride we had yesterday. There were great peals of laughter from all when Andy unwrapped the butter from the newspaper it was in, this was bought a week ago in Turkey. The butter was wrapped in a page 3 of a Turkish newspaper, complete with topless girl! The point is that at the border coming into Iran from Turkey the Iranian customs had given us a hard time searching coaches and luggage for drugs, alcohol, and anything else of a corrupting influence.

We were kept 8 hours while they searched everything twice, once by the morning shift of customs officials, and again by the afternoon shift. Joe's video camera had to be sealed in a strong bag, also with a pack of playing cards (both of a corrupt nature), not to be opened until we had left Iran. They found a supply of 'Encounter Overland' holiday brochures which had a picture of a girl in shorts!! This created a stir of activity, and Andy our courier was taken some kilometres down the road to a higher authority to explain and to convince the authorities that these brochures were not going to be handed out to the people of Iran, but were merely the normal supply of brochures for the company's Kathmandu office. The above mentioned peals of laughter were because we did not know that our butter was wrapped in a page 3 Turkish newspaper, and luckily for us the Iranian customs search of the coach had not been thorough enough to find it, otherwise we would have had to explain we were not smuggling Turkish page 3's into Iran, which might have been difficult, because it could be considered an ingenious method of doing so!

Night at New Lourdes Hotel, Quetta.

Day 42. Sunday Jan 24. Quetta.

It's warm in the sun but cold at night, below freezing, as Quetta is high at altitude 1800 metres. Tea is served in china cups, which is a change from Turkey and Iran where it's served in small glasses. I spent all morning locating the Post Office and finding out how to make phone calls home.

Phoned at 3 p.m. (10 a.m. England).

Yesterday was hilarious, you might say, with our coach continually stopping throughout the day and people running off into the desert clutching rolls of toilet paper and locating the nearest bush or sand dune or rock, including me! Something we all ate in some cafe! Pakistan seems a dirty place generally, and we have to eat outside the hotel sometimes as many hotels don't have restaurants. Had a meal out tonight in a Chinese restaurant. It was all right.

Night at New Lourdes Hotel, Quetta.

Day 43. Monday Jan 25. Quetta to Sukkur.

Andy left us today to drive the big bus as quickly as possible to Kathmandu. So we are now in the small one. Weather hot and dusty all day.

Night at New Pak Inn, Sukkur.

Day 44. Tuesday Jan 26. Sukkur to Bahawalpur.

We stayed here instead of Multan as the roads were so crowded we would not have made Multan in time. The roads here in Pakistan are full of trucks and 'Rocket' buses, the latter being shaped like rockets. All these vehicles look like circus wagons with their bright psychedelic colours and designs. The driving is like a circus too, with narrow main roads, all the buses and trucks constantly overtaking each other, and there is barely room for two vehicles to pass so some one is forced onto the gravel at the side. Safety margins go out of the window!

Night at Hotel Hainare, Bahawalpur.

Day 45. Wednesday Jan 27. Bahawalpur to Lahore.

This morning I discovered I had lost 30 dollars worth of Rupees. The money was in the pocket of my anorak, which I normally carry around with me, but last night I left it in my hotel room while at dinner. Our couriers decided it was better not to report it to the hotel, and accuse the staff, and someone could lose their job, and I couldn't be sure. So I just learned the lesson not to leave money around! We stay in Lahore two nights. Weather is still getting warmer.

Night at International Hotel, Lahore.

Day 46. Thursday Jan 28. Lahore.

The population of Pakistan is 110 million and 75% are illiterate. Most children start school at age 5 and all have to pay something to go to school. However, after one or two years the majority of children, presumably the 75%, leave school. The parents have no motivation for their children because they had none from their own parents, etc. Only 3% of the male population have paid jobs, and the women don't get paid jobs anyway.

Everywhere you see little boys, and big boys, playing cricket on any available open space, and boys running in the fields practising their bowling technique without a ball, as they run. There is plenty of motivation for cricket, but nothing else! Those who are clever enough to go to university and get degrees, leave the country for well paid jobs in Europe. Half of university entrants are girls, but when they leave, they get married, start having children, and never work.

We hired a guide and he took us to the Shalimar Gardens. Lahore was known as the city of gardens, and amongst the six famous Moghul gardens of Lahore, only the Shalimar Garden remains today. It was laid out by Shah Jehan in 1642 as a recreational place for the royal family. There are terraces, lakes, a waterfall and 400 fountains. It might have looked good if it had been cleaned up a bit, and the water had been turned on, but it was rather early in the season!

Night at International Hotel, Lahore.

Days 47-48. Friday-Saturday Jan 29-30. Lahore to Peshawar.

Pakistan is full of surprises. We went on a trip to the top of the Khyber Pass. We were not allowed further as this is the border with Afghanistan. Even so we had to hire

a local guide and he had to get a permit and an armed guard
to accompany us in the bus. We were not allowed to stray
more than 14ft. from the main road, as just outside
Peshawar becomes tribal territory where neither Afghanistan
nor Pakistan has any law controls, and in fact the tribal
people are all smugglers and/or killers. This tribal territory
begins just where the road starts to climb up to the pass,
and at the beginning of this 'No Man's Land' a small market
town has sprung up called Landhi Kotal, it's all shoddy
looking shops including a Marks and Spencer's and St.
Michael's (probably just a well known name stuck up on a
shop front) where all the locals go to buy cheap goods,
mainly all those western items too expensive or impossible
to obtain in Pakistan. The goods are smuggled in from
Afghanistan. The Pakistani government appears to turn a
convenient blind eye to all this! All the tribespeople carry
guns, and there are soldiers with automatic rifles guarding
the road to the pass. Two of these guards fired their guns
into the air – showing off to tourists and blasting
everyone's eardrums – which I thought irresponsible. There
was a separate shop by the roadside that sold guns, but our
coach was not allowed to stop there.

During one of the viewpoint stops we met up with a
coach load of American tourists on a week-end visit from
Saudi Arabia.

Two Nights at Galaxy Hotel, Peshawar.

Day 49. Sunday Jan 31. Peshawar to Lahore.

Night at International Hotel, Lahore.

Day 50-51. Monday-Tuesday Feb 1-2. Lahore to Delhi.

I don't seem to be writing much lately! These are our
first days in India and I haven't got anything good to say
about it so far. Everywhere you go people want your money
– regardless of how nice they are – money is their ulterior
motive. It's worse here than the other countries and it gets
a bit wearing to the patience. You are not allowed to relax
and enjoy India. In itself, Delhi has quite a lot to commend

it – it's reasonably clean in the city – nice parks and a long Mall (like The Mall in London) leading up to India Gate Memorial of an unknown soldier in World War 1 – lots of interesting birds: parakeets, woodpeckers, kites. But you can't do anything without being pestered by street vendors or rickshaw boys, or begging women holding half naked infants. Also shoe-shine boys who want your custom although you just had your shoes cleaned one minute ago (as my friend Lars did yesterday). So your whole time is spent in devising ways to get rid of them quickly. After a time you lose your good humour. If you hire a rickshaw and finally agree a price, during the journey the driver will argue the whole time that he wants more...or he wants to take you to an emporium where there are cheap goods...he will only charge you 10 rupees for the extra journey...he knows good shop...cheap jewellery! Finally your patience wears out, "stop the rickshaw!" and threaten him, "If you don't want to take us to our hotel we'll find another rickshaw!" That usually does the trick.

We did meet two 'nice' ladies at the Golden Temple in Amritsar. Lars and I didn't know if we could go over the bridge to the inner temple in the middle of the lake. Each of the Sikhs was buying a plate of leaves to go in and doing plenty of bowing at many places. These two ladies saw our plight and one who spoke good English explained a little about the temple and that her sister would take us in. So we had a guide who led us, and we saw and heard moving ceremonies, including a reading from the very large original copy of the Sikh holy book, the *Granth Sahib*. There is a ceremony at 10 p.m. and 4 a.m. each day when this book is taken to some safe place ashore each night, and returned the following morning. No money was asked for, it would have been insulting to have offered these ladies a tip. They try to visit the temple once a year to 'cleanse' themselves, all the way from Delhi, an 8 hour journey by train. We ate holy bread coming out of the temple, and walked with bare feet throughout, but it was very clean, one of the few places in India so far that was spotless.

We met a man in the temple area who talked to us for some time about the temple, but he later revealed his ulterior motive...he worked in a bank and wanted to change some of our dollars and pounds 'on the side' to boost his foreign currency account! Would you believe it! He was under-cutting his own bank!

Nights at Ritz Hotel, Amritsar.
Ranjit Hotel, Delhi.

Day 52. Wednesday Feb 3. Delhi.

I haven't yet written about the train journey! In Amritsar, the other day, Carol asked if anyone wanted to travel by train the following morning to Delhi, instead of by our mini-bus, and meet up in our booked hotel later in the day. She thought it might be interesting. Lars, Sato and I decided we would, so Carol booked us first class with reserved seats on the 6 a.m. train.

We set off very early with our packed breakfast from the hotel, and walked to the station. The train didn't have any first class coaches on it, and our coach was definitely bottom class!..with wooden bench seats and our reserved seats already occupied with people and masses of luggage. There was a lady who seemed to be the only one who understood what a reserved seat was. She told two people to move, but one man would not move from his better seat by the window! So Sato had to squeeeze in somewhere else. The journey lasted 8½ hours and was awful! It was cold, and we hadn't brought clothes for such a cold morning, although the sun did shine later in the morning, but we were chilled throughout the whole journey. The locals kept opening the windows, and we kept shutting them when that person got off. There was no heating of course! My bones were sore from the hard seats and I couldn't walk around much due to people sitting on the floor. The smell was unpleasant!

I recommend such a train journey to anyone who wants to see 'India in a Nutshell', if your time is limited...don't stay at the Hilton in Delhi and go on a city tour by tourist bus...just catch the 6 a.m. train from Amritsar to Delhi and travel 2nd (lowest) class, and you'll really find out about India in one day! Stops are frequent...stations seem to have a permanent population camping on the platforms, and here, food and drink vendors were offering their goods...raucous cries of "chai, chai," as the tea boys came along the carriages...I had many drinks and they were hot and warming. I shall hear those cries with every cup of tea I ever drink!

An early morning sight was, just outside suburban stations on waste ground all alongside the railway, people coming and going and squatting, doing their morning toilet..! Well, they have to go somewhere. We were starving hungry when we finally arrived at Delhi – the journey seemed endless. Ross had told us of a Wimpy Bar in Delhi – so we made for it as fast as possible, and enjoyed delicious burger and chips, and next door was Nirula's Ice Cream Parlour...How lucky can you get? It was good! We now felt ready for anything that India might throw at us. We did wonder how Carol had managed to reserve us those seats on that 2nd class train! When we met later that day, she said she couldn't understand it. We still wondered!

Night at Ranjit Hotel, Delhi.

Day 53. Thursday Feb 4. Delhi to Jaipur.

I am now in the Narain Niwas Palace, Jaipur, which is our hotel for the night. It was a hunting lodge of the Raj in the last century and still retains the impression of those days, although now a bit run down. There are monkeys in the trees of the grounds and peacocks in the gardens. In Jaipur there are monkeys all over the town. The waiter (who is also groundsman and houseboy) is dressed as in the last century with red coat and jodhpurs. Today we visited Jaigarh Fort at Amber, 11 kilometres from Jaipur. This was the ancient capital of Jaipur state. The fort was reckoned to be impregnable, its architecture is certainly forbidding. There is a huge 8 metre cannon with ornate barrel – but it was never used in action. Overlooking the main thoroughfare in Jaipur is Hawa Mahal, the Palace of the Winds, a five storey facade in pink sandstone studded with 953 little windows, balconies, and much fine screen work, and it is all only one room deep! The ladies of the royal household used to sit here to catch the breeze 'Hawa' (hence the name) and watch the world go by.

Night at Hotel Narain Niwas Palace. Jaipur.

Days 54-55. Friday-Saturday Feb 5-6. Jaipur to Udaipur.

It's cooler here in Udaipur, which is set beside a lake, and pleasant compared to the arid desert areas we've been through. We hired a local guide and visited Moti Magri or the 'Pearl Hill' which overlooks the lake, and atop the hill is a statue of Rajput hero Maharana Pratap astride his charger Chetak. Also visited Bhartiya Lok Kala Museum to see a show of Rajhasthani puppets.

I had to go to the dentist because I had broken a piece off a tooth eating a hard chip. I was scared! I was taken by a rickshaw boy, who also served as translator. The 'surgery' was just at the back of a shop and looked like a museum piece from the middle ages, with instruments and bottles of potions to match! I tried to be brave. My heart sank when I lay and sank down in the '500 years old' dentist chair and he picked up an instrument! Later, on reflection, I decided he was a good dentist, and knew what he was doing, because he advised me to wait until I returned home – the tooth was quite sound and would not be a problem. He turned out to be correct!

Two Nights at Hotel Anand Bhawan, Udaipur.

Days 56-57. Sunday-Monday Feb 7-8. Udaipur to Jodhpur.

At Jodhpur we walked through the old city streets climbing to Meherangarth Fort where a guide was provided to show us round the museum. On the way down near the top, we got into conversation with a man standing outside his house...he invited us in – Carol, Lars, and myself, to meet his family, and we sat cross-legged on the floor drinking tea and looking at a daughter's school books. The house was very basic, but clean. He built the house himself, with only two rooms and yard where the parents sleep out under the stars – it hardly ever rains here. We saw another daughter Anita's collection of foreign currency notes, to which we added a few more. This was a very enjoyable episode...he was lucky because he had a job, working for the water board.

We had a very enjoyable buffet dinner at our hotel complete with orchestra and dancing girls.

I find the daytime sun unbearable...I can't get used to it...all I want to do is get in the shade. When we get to Nepal it will be less hot as it is higher.

Two Nights at Hotel Ajit Bhawan, Jodhpur.

Days 58-59. Tuesday-Wednesday Jan 9-10. Jophpur to Jaisalmer.

Jaisalmer is an exotic old city and fort, 'a medieval fantasy in the middle of the desert', according to the guide books. Old cities and forts in India, of which there are many, are all well kept and reasonably clean, but still the towns attached to the old cities, where all the people live and shop etc. are all shabby and dirty and smelly.

Here we drove 30 kilometres out into the desert to watch the sun set over the sand dunes and take photos. On the drive back, when it was dark, we stopped to star gaze in the desert night sky, and wonder at the magnificence of the universe!

Two nights at Hotel Neeraj, Jaisalmer.

Day 60. Thursday Feb 11. Jaisalmer to Bikaner.

Bikaner is just another dirty town with fort.

Night at Thar Hotel, Bikaner.

Days 61-62. Friday-Saturday Feb 12-13. Bikaner to Jaipur.

We are now back in Jaipur again staying in the same hotel that was once a hunting lodge, having travelled in a loop known as 'the Golden Triange'. This refers to the area south of Delhi where many wonders of India are situated.

We visited a very interesting outdoor observatory called *Jantar Mantar*, built in 1728 and well preserved, for plotting the stars, the seasons, eclipses, and for astrology. The giant sundial with its 30 metre high gnomon is the most striking of the instruments, and tells the time with great accuracy. I took a picture of Aries.

Two Nights at Hotel Narain Niwas Palace, Jaipur.

Day 63. Sunday Feb 14. Jaipur to Agra.

On our journey today we stopped at Keoladio National Park, which is mainly a bird sanctuary. The 'finest water bird reserve in the world', according to our guide, who we hired with punt (for quietness) and punter, for 1½ hours. Compared to what I've seen of other bird reserves it was wonderful – saw lots of exotic birds – Herons, Egrets, Geese, Harriers, Cranes, Lapwing, Plovers, Owl, Swallow, Kingfisher, Painted Stork, and Vultures which are all over India.

Night at Hotel Amar, Agra.

Day 64. Monday Feb 15. Agra.

We all rose early to see the sun rise over the Taj Mahal...it's magnificent! But...my top list of monuments so far is:

1. Ramses II Temple at Abu Simbel. Egypt.
2. Taj Mahal, Agra, India.
3. Karnak Temple, Luxor, Egypt.
4. Valley of the Kings, Luxor, Egypt.
5. Golden Temple, Amritsar, India.
6. Petra Lost City, Jordan.

All six very impressive, although Valley of the Kings has many separate tombs. The Ramses Temple tops my list because of its sheer size and magnificence, also I'm impressed by the magnitude of the modern day task of moving it further up the mountain to avoid the waters of the flooded plateau when the Aswan High Dam project was completed.

We had a conducted tour of Agra fort. Shah Jahan built the Taj Mahal in 1630 as a tomb for his beloved wife Mumtaz Mahal who had just died in her 14th childbirth. It was completed in 1652. He then started planning his own tomb which was to be a replica on the opposite bank of the river, but in black marble (the Taj Mahal is in white). However, he was deposed by his penny-pinching son Aurangzeb, in an effort to stop his architectural extravagance. He was put in prison in Agra Fort where he could always see his wife's tomb. He died in prison in 1665. It is a lovely view from the fort looking out to the Taj not far away. A little sad, that story! His tomb rests at the side of his wife's in the Taj.

Agra is full of hotels – bottom, medium, and top end, and there are masses of tourists, all taking photographs of the Taj Mahal. Kodak must make a fortune every day from the Taj Mahal alone! I returned on my own at 4 p.m. to see and take photos with the fountains on, which were supposed to be turned on at four o'clock, but with typical Indian 'misinformation', they were turned on today at 3.30 and off at four o'clock, so I just missed it, although I took some good reflections in the lake.

Misinformation is a way of life here. I ought to be used to it after all this time travelling through Asia, but it still takes me by surprise because there are so many variations of it. One gets caught 'off guard'. The first thing we do when shown to our hotel room is check for towels, soap, toilet paper, lights, toilet flushing, door lock, when will hot water be turned on? sheets look clean? This is before we let the porter leave the room. I'm somewhat organised in this respect as this is my 40th hotel so far on this trip! Never are all the above things O.K. so I make a quick decision as to what is essential, because you'd do nothing else the whole evening if you insisted everything was correct. Today we decided to go for towels, which were missing. "Yes sir, two towels," and off he rushed. Half an hour later I went down to reception. "Where are the towels for room 108 that your man said he would get?" There was excited talking by 4 staff and a telephone call, all in Hindi of course. "Right away Sir." So I went back to the room thinking we'd get some towels soon. It was about 5 p.m... I should have known better! I returned to reception after another half hour. "Where are my towels?" "Sorry Sir, we've had lots of groups in today and haven't any. I promise you sir, you will have towels by 8 o'clock," whereupon he shook my hand as if it was a gentleman's agreement. After dinner at 8.30 there were no towels. After making a fuss for the next half hour, we got them at 9 o'clock. There are things that can go wrong which you find out about after using the room a little – like the toilet cistern filling up with water and the ballcock valve sometimes turning off the water and sometimes not, and you finding the bathroom flooded – or you having a shower and the water doesn't run away because the drain is blocked. Lars usually fixes the plumbing, as he's rather good at it, and it's quicker to do it yourself rather than call the staff.

Night at Hotel Amar, Agra.

Day 65. Tuesday Feb 16. Agra to Khajuraho.

On our route today we visited Fatehpur Sikri, a perfectly preserved example of a great Moghul city, which was the capital of the Moghul empire from 1570.

At Khajuraho we visited the site of many temples built during the Chandella period around 960–1050 A.D. The outsides of the temple walls are almost completely covered with sculptures of people doing every day activities: ploughing, feasting, playing musical instruments, dancing, and sex, the last of which it is more famous for. Most of the temples are dedicated to the gods *Vishnu and Shiva.* The people only stayed about a hundred years, and quite why they chose such a dismal and remote site is unknown, as is the reason for their sudden demise.

Night at Hotel Payal, Khajuraho.

Day 66. Wednesday Feb 17. Khajuraho to Varanasi.

This city Varanasi was called Benares when the British were here and is the holiest city of the Hindus, where they make their pilgrimage, and each day along a 2 kilometre stretch of the sacred River Ganges, untold numbers of Hindus cleanse themselves of sin in the murky, muddy, dirty waters from properly constructed bathing ghats, which are steps down to the water's edge from the high water mark to the low water mark. It's quite a distance between these two for dry and monsoon periods. We hired a boat, boatman, and guide called Uncle to view this activity from the river in time for the sunrise at 6.30, for it is at sunrise when the cleansing action is most effective! They wade out tentatively from the bank – men in bathing trunks, women with more clothing on, and duck themselves under, with their chidren, and brush their teeth as well.

A dead cow floated past by us with 3 vultures balanced on it having breakfast. (The cow is a sacred animal and a person must not harm or kill a cow in India). The local people use this same stretch of river to do their laundry for there are as many people washing clothes as washing themselves. Laundry companies must also use it, for you see scores of colourful shawls all laid out together in rows on the ghats to dry. You can imagine it is a stunning and vivid sight as viewed from a boat moving along this stretch of river. I just sat and stared as the sun came up from across this very wide river.

Just to add to the drama of the morning, in between the bathing ghats are funeral ghats where the dead are cremated on huge piles of tree timber. Like the bathing, this is a very holy place to be cremated and Hindus will spend lots of money to have their bodies cremated here and ashes scattered on the river. There was a body waiting to be burned while we were there, bound up in white... when we came back the other way it had gone. We were not allowed to take photos anywhere near the burning ghat.

Varanasi must be the noisiest, busiest place in India, although I never thought it possible to be busier than Delhi. Walking along the street is so noisy, and it's so difficult to avoid all the bicycles, bicycle rickshaws, and motor rickshaws, that it is better to hire a rickshaw and let someone else dodge the traffic for you. You need to be really motivated to go shopping anywhere here. It is also a centre for the silk trade and we visited a silk weaving factory.

We met an Encounter Overland (same as Sundowners) group in their overland truck, going the other way i.e. Kathmandu to Cairo. We stopped and chatted about what it was like going through Asia, as they had only started their trip a few days ago. They were not staying in hotels like us, but camping.

Night at Hotel Pradeep, Varanasi.

Day 67. Thursday Feb 18. Varanasi.

Yesterday's scene at sunrise over the Ganges was the most spectacular human sight I have seen so far on this trip – the ancient monuments were great, but this was a human spectacle. I have just learned that if you can manage to die in Varanasi it only costs 200 rupees (£5) to be burned on the ghat, but coming from elsewhere it costs a lot more. My daughter Jill and husband came to this part of India – I wonder if they came here?

Our deaf friend Sato went out with members of the local deaf club and they took him to see an afternoon cremation. For some reason there was a disturbance with police using their sticks (bamboo poles of 3 feet long and 1 inch thick) and the whole thing made him feel sick! I have seen the police using these sticks on moped riders who, in a traffic jam, try to get past the traffic cop who is holding up their line of traffic. Varanasi is a sight worth seeing, but I was glad to get away...it wears you out!

Night at Hotel Pradeep, Varanasi.

Day 68. Friday Feb 19. Varanasi to Sunauli, Nepal.

The Day we Left India

We travelled all day from Varanasi – 329 kilometres – and arrived at the India–Nepal border late afternoon. It was a typical Indian village – dirty, with many cows and goats roaming the streets. We waited in the coach amid the hustle and bustle of late afternoon village life – lots of people with loads on their heads walking towards the border. Why were they going to Nepal? Emigrating? Working? Visiting relatives? It wasn't our business I suppose. Carol, our courier, had gone into the immigration office, which looked just like any other shop in the 'High Street'.

While waiting in the coach I saw in a shop what I thought looked like chocolate bars. Chocolate! I hadn't seen a bar of chocolate for weeks! months! it seemed like years! I suppose in the areas I'd been through it was too hot for chocolate, but here on the border with Nepal, where the altitude is higher, it's cooler and suitable for the enjoyment of chocolate. I can't go in the shop as we're not allowed out of the coach to wander, as we often do for shopping etc. at most stops in villages, because here we have to be ready to file in to the immigration office altogether as a group. This village of Belhiya is maybe dirtier and dustier than most others we've seen, so we wouldn't want to shop here anyway, but chocolate bars are wrapped, so maybe later!

We were eventually called into the immigration office, a room with a couple of tables and chairs, with an official sitting behind one of the tables. The room looked as if it hadn't been decorated for a very long time; a stone floor, no carpet, dusty, a few travel posters on the walls...torn and dirty!

The usual formalities:

"Nationality?" He had my passport in front of him, so he should have known.

"British," I said.

"Have you enjoyed your stay in India?"

Well...! What a question! What could I say to that? Could I really say it was lovely? Was all that I'd dreamed about? That I enjoyed every minute of my three weeks stay in India?

It's impossible to describe what effect India has on you. It hits very hard on the senses. The sight of all the poverty, the smells, the noise in the streets, the close proximity of too many people in the bazaars, sacred cows wandering aimlessly, apparently belonging to no one. Underfed cats and dogs asleep in the gutters. Yet it's the people that make up the country. The people who are mainly poor, can't read or write – maybe they're happy in their simple way of life, and according to reports, living conditions in some parts of Africa are worse!

The people who come into contact with the tourists always want your money, and they are devious in the ways of getting as much as they can. I can't blame them if it makes their life a bit easier. In the large towns like Delhi you get the beggars – often young women holding a near naked baby, following you for money; people trying to sell you picture postcards or jewellery, "Buy ten for good bargain," "Be my friend and buy some,"; the small boys who pester you to clean your shoes; the rickshaw boys; taxi men trying to get your custom. All these people are very persistent and will not take no for an answer – they will follow you and pester you. If you do want their services, their price will always be too high, so you bargain, and a price is finally agreed. But this is no 'gentleman's agreement', the concept just doesn't exist! for during and at the end of the rickshaw drive, or cleaning of shoes, they will say the agreed money is not enough, and want more, all the time. We have learnt to resist this pressure, with good humour, but it's not easy.

So when you are in town you can: 1. Ignore them, by not appearing to notice their presence, even when followed. 2. Say "No thank you," and keep saying it again and again while being followed. 3. Try reasoned argument..."Do you understand English?" – "Right! – Do you understand the word 'No'?" – "Good, well, no I don't want any, so please leave me alone." 4. Be downright rude and shout at them to "Get out of my way!" This last is not recommended as losing your temper doesn't make for an enjoyable holiday. Sometimes, if I'm fed up with pestering, I walk extremely fast, cross roads, duck under arches, into shops, not giving them a chance to catch me up, let alone speak, until they give up – really like playing a game! Ross, our 'Kiwi' courier, only ever used one method...he just ignored them as if they didn't exist! But I found that method a bit too rude, perhaps if I'd stayed in India longer I'd use that method more! This is all part of the experience of India, and we must keep our good humour.

Sometimes we meet ordinary people, off the tourist

routes, where they're not after your money, not 'geared up for the rip-off', usually in the villages when buying fruit, or drinks, or Samosa at a roadside kitchen – where a simple conversation, aided by sign language, reveals that these people are ordinary, nice, with families, making the best of their meagre lifestyle, and really lovely people.

So to understand what India is like, you need to experience the SIGHTS, the SOUNDS, and the SMELLS, right there in India at close quarters.

"Have you enjoyed your stay in India?" the immigration official had asked.

"Yes...it was very interesting...I learnt a lot." This was the only answer I could summon. It didn't seem to matter anyway, the official just stamped my passport, and seemed not to have heard me...

We were soon finished with the formalities, and were back on the coach and driving across the border into Nepal, where a hotel was soon found with vacancies just a few hundred yards away called the Manti Hotel. This was hardly a hotel by western standards. It ranked alongside the Dak Bungalow at Dalbantin, which was just over the border into Pakistan from Iran (Day 40). There were bare concrete floors, unpainted walls, bedsteads without mattresses, no furniture, a toilet of sorts with a shower that actually worked if you didn't mind standing bare foot on a dirty concrete floor, no outside windows – only one onto a landing. We never saw much of all this economy of style because it was nearly dark on arrival, and there was a power cut almost immediately after turning on the light. A candle had to be set up on the floor, also a mosquito coil.

I had told Carol, our courier, about the chocolate bars I thought I had seen in a shop opposite the immigration office in Belhiya (India), and she, like me, liked the idea of getting some chocolate. She had in fact spoken to me a few days ago about how she missed her choc. and Mars bars. No one else seemed interested, all the others liked their whisky, rum, and vodka. So this is how Carol and I plotted to go back across the border, under cover of darkness to smuggle back some chocolate – if it existed! She thought the border post guards were very relaxed, and only a short time before, while it was still light enough, we could see from the hotel that there were still people walking across the border in both directions.

We had put on our dirtiest clothes, my hat pulled right down to cover my pale face, and she her black scarf worn in Iran. All was set! We'd meet the others on our return at a restaurant near the hotel. There were two border posts with gates to cross, one Nepalese, one Indian, with about 50 yards of No Man's Land between. We were not really committing a crime as our Indian visas were valid for multiple entries, although our Nepalese visas were valid only for a single entry, which of course we had used up a couple of hours previously. No turning back now! We were already walking along the three hundred yards to the first border post. It was now dark with a few faint lights coming from buildings by the first post – oil lamps probably, remembering there was a power cut. Open the gate...we went through...shut the gate...walk 50 yards...there were two people coming towards the second gate from the Indian side...they reached the gate first...keep our nerve..! "Don't say thank you," Carol whispered, "we're supposed to be locals." They actually held open the gate for us, but we didn't say a word...we were through! We weren't challenged! There was no sign of anyone near the border post buildings, so we went on to the shop looking for chocolate. It WAS chocolate I had seen! We bought six Cadbury's Milk Bars each, and managed to resist eating more than one bar each – we were just about to have dinner. Isn't life good sometimes? But we had to get back to Nepal, to the restaurant to meet the others. The return across the border was no problem, no one challenged us, and we met the others who were all drinking beer awaiting our return from our little adventure.

The hotel was still in darkness on our return from the restaurant, Power cuts were a nuisance, and I hadn't got round to writing a card for my sister Doris's birthday. I wrote it in the candle light and decided to get up early, leave the hotel at 6.30, walk across the border again and post the card in India (I still had an Indian postage stamp). Carol had identified a post box for me on our excursion this evening! I chanced a shower in the toilet in the near darkness, and went to bed in my sleeping bag on the bare canvas stretched bedstead. The others in my room, Lars and Sato, were already snoring...it was midnight...and very cold...too cold for the mosquitoes that were supposed to be around!

In the morning breakfast was to be at 7 a.m. so I left the hotel at 6.30 and headed for India once again, mixing with all the hustle and bustle of people going about their business – people getting on and off buses, breakfast vendors – the ever present sacred cows wandering aimlessly, also goats, dogs, cats, and pigs all nibbling at rubbish. All these animals had, it seemed, as much right to be on the road and sidewalks (I can't think of another word to describe the dirt ground at the side of the road), as the traffic and humans. I don't think anyone even noticed me dodging all the above, and this time, in daylight, I found I could easily duck under the two check point gates at each side of the border. There were no problems, so I posted my card and returned, still no problem, and was back in time for 7 a.m. breakfast.

The weather is decidedly cooler in Nepal at this higher altitude.

Night at Manti Hotel, Sunauli, Nepal.

Day 69. Saturday Feb 20. Sunauli to Pokhara.

It's even cooler here. Pokhara is quite nice, beside a lake and you can see Annapurna in the distance covered in snow. It's getting quite mountainous now after the flat plains of India. We all got out to the lake early at 6.30 to view and take photos of Annapurna in the sunrise. Mount Everest is not visible from here. Today is the official end of this *Cairo to Kathmandu* trip, but we are a day late having stopped at Petra, Jordan, which was not scheduled. The intention was to make up the day by missing Pokhara and going straight to Kathmandu from the border, but *Sundowners* didn't mind us being a day late, and we passengers didn't have any urgent plans in Kathmandu, so we stopped in Pokhara, to arrive in Kathmandu tomorrow Sunday.

Night at The Hungry Eye, Pokhara.

Day 70. Sunday Feb 21. Pokhara to Kathmandu.

Last Day of Cairo to Kathmandu Overland Trip

Today was a long slow climb through mountain passes with spectacular scenery and weather cooler.

Sato, our deaf Japanese friend, left our trip at the border yesterday, where he met up with a local deaf group. He is staying with them for a month to teach tailoring, before going home to Melbourne, where he lives. Unfortunately he will be on another holiday in April when I pass through Melbourne with Pat, so we can't call on him.

I am sharing a room here in Kathmandu with Lars, until he flies home next Saturday. Joe and Julie fly to Bangkok next Sunday, where they join another trip to Chiang Mai – they are great travellers, as they will have been away for 11 months when they eventually get home to Brisbane. So I have one week here with company, and another week on my own. We had a farewell dinner this evening, saying good-bye to our couriers Carol and Ross, and surprise...! They presented us with $205 U.S.Dollars each, which was the amount underspent from the food and accommodation fund. We were well pleased! We will still see them around as their office 'Himalayan Encounters' is adjacent to the hotel.

Night at Kathmandu Guest House, Kathmandu.

Stage 3
Kathmandu to Bangkok

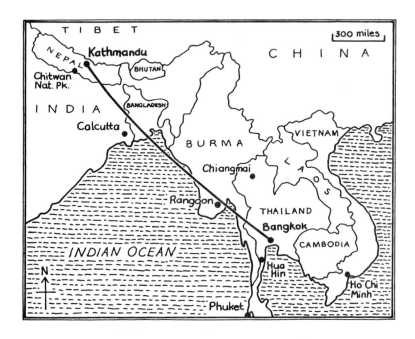

I had 3 weeks to spare between the end of the Cairo to Kathmandu overland trip and the beginning of the Bangkok to Bali trip. I decided to spend 2 weeks in Kathmandu and 1 week in Bangkok. Distance was 1,369 miles.

Day 71. Monday Feb 22. Kathmandu.

Today I received letters from all the family and was pleased to hear everyone's news.

I haven't done much here today – just winding down after 10 weeks of travelling. Walked to Durbar Square in the old city, which is just like a time warp from the Middle Ages. The square is packed with houses, shops, strange statues, monuments and weird temples. The roads are cobblestones. But the strange thing was that the local people didn't fit the picture – most of them wore jeans and T-shirt, so I came to the conclusion that either these people were trying to be like westerners by imitating their dress, or these 20th century Nepalese had pressed the button in a time machine that transported them back to 16th century Kathmandu. There were some people who fitted the 16th century though, which made the time machine theory very plausible...reminds me of *H.G. Wells The Time Machine.* I don't know how I fit into all this as an outside observer! Perhaps I'd better shut my diary for today!

Night at Kathmandu Guest House, Kathmandu.

Day 72. Tuesday Feb 23. Kathmandu.

Lars and I got up early yet again, this time to see the sun rise from the Swayambhunath Temple which is on top of a hill a few kilometres out of town. It's commonly called Monkey Temple because there are swarms of them over the temple and grounds. The sunrise was a bit of a let down because it was too misty, also cold! The monkeys were having a good time running and jumping up the sides of temples and climbing up bunting strings. They just seemed to be in high spirits and were doing it naturally and not for the benefit of the humans, as they do at zoos. The temple is a symbol of Kathmandu and appears on tourist brochures. The monkeys did not harass us so I assume they had an ample food supply. The temple was worth seeing but we didn't see the view because of the mist.

Night at Kathmandu Guest House, Kathmandu.

Day 73. Wednesday Feb 24. Kathmandu.

Lars and I visited the Thai Embassy to see about my visa, then on to Patan the second city of the valley, which also has a Durbar Square, and like the one in Kathmandu, has a weird assortment of temples and buildings. This square is across the river and less than 5 kilometres from the Durbar Square in Kathmandu. There is a good Handicrafts Cooperative Center here where prices of goods are actually marked and are very reasonable. The price is not normally marked on goods throughout the Middle East and Asia – one has to bargain! I took a photo of the two young lady assistants and promised to send them a print.

Night at Kathmandu Guest House, Kathmandu.

Day 74. Thursday Feb 25. Kathmandu.

Bhaktapur is the third major city in the valley, and like the other two, also has a Durbar Square full of temples and statues. Lars and I went by local bus today and it took 1 hour to cover the 14 kilometres and we were packed in like sardines with people hanging on the back as is usual. It was agony for me because I was ill all day, a different illness from my previous ones because I couldn't eat anything. By the time we wanted to set off back, I couldn't face the prospect of another such bus ride, as I felt worse, so I paid for a taxi at 150 Rupees. The bus cost 3 Rupees (4 pence). The taxi ride of 14 kilometres was still cheap by English standards but I've been out in this part of the world so long now that I thought it expensive!

Night at Kathmandu Guest House, Kathmandu.

Day 75. Friday Feb 26. Kathmandu.

Walked with Lars to the other side of town to pick up spectacles he had ordered, also to pick up my visa from the Thai Embassy.

Night at Kathmandu Guest House, Kathmandu.

Day 76. Saturday Feb 27. Kathmandu.

In the afternoon I went to the airport with Lars to see him off. Now there are three of our original group of five.

Night at Kathmandu Guest House, Kathmandu.

Day 77. Sunday Feb 28. Kathmandu.

I spent all the morning and early afternoon changing

rooms at the hotel, as I wanted a cheaper room now I'm alone. This last week has cost me US$8.50 a day sharing, now I have a single room costing US$10 a day, not such a good room, but adequate. This is the most expensive hotel we have used so far since Cairo, as through the Middle East and Asia a twin room often cost around $US2 or 3, so we have been rather spoilt for hotel costs. The hotels in Lausanne and Paris cost around $US60, and they were Daily Telegraph half price special offers. All the countries we've visited seem to have dollars as their unofficial base currency, so I don't think in pounds much. A lot of hotels, including this one, publish room rates in $US, and some of them, the ones in Syria, will only accept payment in $US. Every one wants foreign currency, right from the smallest shopkeeper to the big business. They mainly want dollars, but the well off and middle class want sterling as well. Consequently there is a black market in money changing, giving better exchange rates than the banks give. Incredibly the black market money changers operate unhindered at border crossings, often in front of customs and bank buildings. It's illegal, but somehow it's allowed to happen.

I said good-bye to Joe and Julie, as they went off to the airport. Now there is only one! I'm on my own again!

Night at Kathmandu Guest House, Kathmandu.

Days 78-79. Monday-Tuesday March 1-2. Kathmandu.

Today, Monday, I have booked up to go on a 3 day safari to Chitwan National Park which is 175 kms. from Kathmandu, I leave on Wednesday.

Various mundane matters:

I have had 2 eggs for breakfast almost continuously on the overland trip, usually fried, with Pita bread. If we've not liked the look of the food offered, they've always got eggs! Lately in Kathmandu, I have been giving my stomach a rest by having only porridge and coffee, and for lunch having soup, bread, and Lassi, which is whisked up yoghurt and comes as a drink. Others in the group had it in India and Pakistan, but I've only just got round to trusting it, and in fact liking it. Our courier insisted I ate proper yoghurt throughout our journey in Iran when I was ill. In some countries there wasn't much choice of food, like in Iran it was *chelo kebab* or *shish kebab*, and nothing else. In Pakistan and India it was *lamb masala* or *chicken masala*, which is like meat and vegetable stew, always hot with chilli but barely warm in temperature. I always ate 2 or 3 oranges, mandarins, or bananas a day which are all very cheap, also guava fruit, the cheapest at 6 pence per kilo. You can always get fresh fruit juice very cheaply per glass, I have pineapple or carrot, or a mixture. You can watch them put the fruit into a mechanical squeezer – I enjoyed these!

Sometimes we stayed in better class hotels where there was a choice of western style dishes – steaks, chickens etc. I remember one meal I liked, 'Singaporean Steak', which was minced beef, like a Wiener Schnitzel, with pineapple slice. The price of food here in Kathmandu is more expensive than all the other countries we've been through, but then we've been spoilt, because it's still cheap, for example I pay $US1 for breakfast; about the same for a snack lunch; $US3 or 4 for two courses and coffee for dinner. It's relatively expensive here because there are so many tourists: American, Australian, New Zealanders, British, French, and German. They are mostly young and look like the people you see at ski resorts in Europe. It certainly is trendy to come to Kathmandu! However, I don't feel out of place as there is a sprinkling of older people.

I've had to buy lightweight trousers and shorts for the heat in Thailand. I had to have them made to measure as the only ones in the shops which all the young people wear are outrageous, ballooning, and multi-coloured... unsuitable for an elderly gentleman! It was no problem finding a tailor as you cannot go far without seeing a clothing shop with sewing machines always at the back. Kathmandu is a maze of side roads and back streets, all full of restaurants, trekking agencies, safari agencies, white water rafting agencies, jewellers, bookshops, carpet shops, postal and shipping agents, clothing shops, and photo shops. Prices are astronomical for shipping carpets, so I won't be buying any, unfortunately, as they are cheap and of good quality!

There was no political trouble during our trip across the Middle East and Asia, only in Cairo and Delhi after leaving. In Cairo, the week after we left, a bomb exploded, killing someone. Soon after leaving Delhi there was trouble over an anti-government demonstration, and there still is trouble, as we heard the government had advised tourists to stay away. Syria and Jordan were fine, you wouldn't know there had been trouble, these countries both sharing a border with Iraq.

Nights at Kathmandu Guest House, Kathmandu.

Day 80. Wednesday March 3. Kathmandu to Chitwan.

I left the hotel at 6.20 a.m. to catch the 7 o'clock tourist bus, which was good by Asian standards, and with a reserved seat. Arrived Chitwan for 2 o'clock lunch. There are 6 of us on this safari, and in the afternoon we went on a nature walk, followed by a bullock cart ride, fording a river to visit an elephant breeding centre where all elephants are kept in semi-captivity. There were 24 elephants, some babies. In the evening we saw a Nepalese folk dancing display, followed by dinner.

Night at Safari Lodge, Chitwan National Park.

Day 81. Thursday March 4. Chitwan.

This morning we made an early start and were taken by jeep to board a dug-out canoe, with 2 guides and boatman to do bird watching, also saw deer, antelope and a crocodile after leaving the canoe, then on walking safari and bullock cart back to lodge. The jeep and bullock cart both ford the river here which is about 2 feet deep at the crossing points. There are tigers, leopards, and lots of rhino, but we haven't seen them yet. My group consists of a young Japanese couple and three Canadians from Grande Prairie, which happens to be on my itinerary going across Canada. They are brother, sister and girl friend. I am writing this in the lodge garden, where it is very peaceful and quiet sitting in the shade during siesta time out of the mid-day sun. The temperature is 30°c in the shade.

7 p.m. This afternoon we have been on an Elephant safari looking for rhinoceros – two people per elephant plus the elephant boy. My elephant weighed 6 ton and was very well trained and gentle, helping with her trunk to push away branches that may have swung back at us. We forded many rivers and got quite close to two rhinos. My companion was Gilles, one of the Canadians, who took video film with great difficulty. It lasted 1½ hours, and was O.K after getting used to the height above the ground, and letting yourself go with the jolts, as when riding a camel, although I refused camel rides both in Egypt and India. We travelled through thick bush, sometimes higher than eye level. These elephants are kept in captivity at night – tied to a stake with a chain round one ankle. Each day from 9 till 4 the elephant boys take their charges out in the bush for grazing, returning in time to take tourists on safari.

After dinner we all went to the local village Mustard Seed Treading festival, where all the villagers and children dance in a long line back and forth on the mustard harvest, singing as well, while others kept piling on the mustard plants. We were made to join in as well, but only stayed half an hour, although the villagers go on half through the night finishing with a feast.

Night at Safari Lodge, Chitwan National Park.

Day 82. Friday March 5. Chitwan to Kathmandu.

Up early this Morning to go bird watching before breakfast, also saw another crocodile. My three Canadian friends gave me a lift in their hired car back to Kathmandu.

Arrived back in hotel to receive telephone message from Carol that my mother had died on Tuesday – Pat had phoned on Wednesday after I had left for the Safari. I thought I would have to go home...and maybe get back to Bangkok to join the overland trip leaving on 14th March, or even cancel that trip and come out to Bali with Pat on the 3rd April...? But when I phoned Pat, she said there was no point in coming home as she and my sister Doris had done all that was necessary, funeral arrangements etc. So I stayed, and felt very guilty about it...! I was talking about my problem to another guest in the hotel and he posed the question: "What would your mother have wanted you to do – carry on with your trip, or go home to her funeral...?" That made me feel a bit better as I'm sure she would have said, "Carry on," and I had done my best for her when she was alive, which was really more important! But leaving Pat and Doris to cope with everything..? But then Pat had insisted I stayed and carried on with my trip..! I felt depressed, and helpless with only a few minutes on the phone to talk about such matters.

Night at Kathmandu Guest House, Kathmandu.

Day 83. Saturday March 6. Kathmandu.

Today I got ready for my departure tomorrow, shopping etc. for things needed in Thailand.

Night at Kathmandu Guest House.

Day 84. Sunday March 7. Kathmandu to Bangkok.

I had a taxi ordered for 7 a.m. so it was too early for breakfast. An Indian lady asked me at the last minute if she could share my taxi. I was thinking that she would also share the cost, but she never offered and I never asked!
Andy, who drove the second bus on the Cairo to Kathmandu trip, was also booked on my flight to Bangkok – he was going back home on leave to Perth – so I arranged to meet him at the airport and we would travel together. The flight went like clockwork, no problems and only 10 minutes late.

The temperature in Bangkok is 34°c with high humidity. It saps all my energy! Especially as I was wearing all my winter clothes, plus anorak to keep my checked-in luggage down to 20 kilos, which it was precisely. I couldn't send my surplus clothes home from Nepal as shipping costs were too high, but here in Bangkok it's cheaper so I'll be sending a large parcel home.

Night at New Fuji Hotel, Bangkok.

Day 85. Monday March 8. Bangkok.

Today I just rested and went swimming in the hotel pool.

Night at New Fuji Hotel. Bangkok.

Days 86-90. Tuesday-Saturday March 9-13. Bangkok.

I changed hotels today to the Swan, which is cheaper, but adequate, also with swimming pool. It's only 300 metres from the New Fuji so I did the change over in a tuk-tuk. The swan costs $US22, the New Fuji $US32. I will stay 5 nights then change back to the New Fuji on Sunday to join the Bangkok to Bali overland group.

My room at the Swan overlooks the swimming pool and I have a balcony. Sometimes I swim and sit by the pool. A few hundred yards away looms the tower block of the Oriental Hotel which I remember visiting in 1985 to catch the river bus. The Bangkok Palace Hotel where I stayed in that year is a long way the other side of town. I have been to the Siam Centre restaurant 'Highlights' which I remembered from '85. The Siam Centre itself has been vastly upgraded – stainless steel everywhere, escalators, cinemas, and restaurants including McDonald's and Pizza Hut. The 'Highlights' restaurant has also gone upmarket, but prices are still comparable to those downtown, where I'm staying. It's large, with the inevitable T.V. in one section, and another section with a band group and singer. The place is big enough to sit away from the loud speakers and feel comfortable in the ear. It's a decidedly much smarter restaurant...wish you were all here! To get there I have to take a 15 minute bus journey which costs 3½ Baht (10p). I've been there a few times for dinner this week.

The Thai people of downtown Bangkok are generally very smartly dressed, women wear mini-skirts and men are often in white shirts and dark trousers. Even the street traders are quite smart. The 3-wheel tuk-tuks look sparkling new and the local buses are as comfortable as you would expect in the west. Downtown, where I'm staying, is full of tourists as most of the big chain hotels are here near the river, but in the Siam Centre area I don't see any at all, and on the buses I use, I'm the only tourist, but I don't feel uncomfortable, people don't stare as if you're from another planet, like they do in India and such places.

8 a.m. Thursday. I have just received a scribbled message that was stuck on a board in the hotel foyer. It reads: 'A BABY GIRL. OK. FROM JILL' I expect Tim (Jill's husband) had phoned to say that Jill had just had a baby. My mother dies...and her great grandchild is born exactly one week later!

11 p.m. Friday. There has been steady rain for the last 3 hours here so the temperature has dropped considerably from its normal 34/35°c. Today I decided I'd had enough of my on-off illness, I had diarrhoea again this morning, and I had stomach pains a few days ago, and it's been going on too long...so I found a medical centre...result is that I have Salmonella poisoning and have to take sulpha drugs for 2 weeks, then a few days later report to the nearest hospital to make sure that I'm clear, and if not, carry on with the drugs. I don't feel sorry for myself, and I'm not too bad really. I've got too many things to think of to do with my future travels!

I took a bus to the other side of town to have a look round the Indra Regent Hotel, which we often visited in 1985 for breakfast, also to look round the street markets nearby.

Back in the hotel I met a young fellow by the swimming pool who is going round the world in 4 weeks. He has 6 stop-overs and got in from Sydney today. We had plenty to talk about, his trip being vastly different from mine. He's a motor mechanic from Cowes on the Isle of Wight.

5 Nights at the Swan Hotel, Bangkok.

Stage 4
Bangkok to Bali

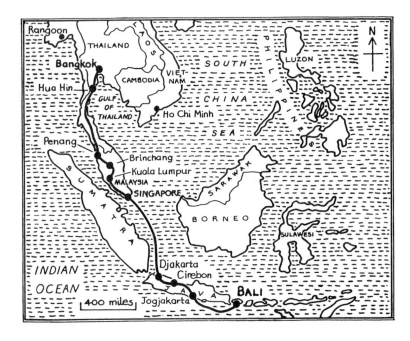

On this section I travelled with a group organized by Trailfinders, a London travel company, and led by a tour manager. There were 18 people and we travelled by train, bus, and 2 flights. Distance was 2,593 miles, and it took 21 days.

Day 91. Sunday March 14. Bangkok.

I'm all packed up and waiting to check out of the Swan hotel, then check in at the New Fuji, where I hope to meet the tour leader. This is my 48th hotel so far since leaving London exactly 3 months ago.

We had a tour meeting in the local pub. and met our companions for the next three weeks. Our tour leader Steve gave out itinerary and hotels information. The hotels all seem good class, and he explained that the tour has moved up market in recent years, merely dictated by the sort of people who go on the tour. They are definitely not back packing types, as I thought they might be! Age groups from mid-twentics upwards. My room mate is a fellow from Southampton aged 65.

Night at New Fuji Hotel, Bangkok.

Day 92. Monday March 15. Bangkok.

Went with tour group on organized excursion visiting the major sights including many Wots and the Grand Palace. We hired a boat for the travelling on the Chao Phraya River and I saw the same sights as we saw in 1985, except then we were unable to see the Grand Palace.

Night at New Fuji Hotel, Bangkok.

Day 93. Tuesday March 16. Bangkok to Hua Hin.

Departed Bangkok by hired coach to Hua Hin. This is luxury coach travel with air conditioning and comfortable seats. En Route we visited Petchburi to see a hilltop palace and temple. Arrived Hua Hin late afternoon to a good class air-conditioned hotel.

Night at Supermitr Hotel, Hua Hin.

Day 94. Wednesday March 17. Hua-Hin.

I chose not to go on the organized beach excursion, so wandered round the town and harbour. It's a fishing town so I watched fish, squid and shrimps being washed and loaded onto lorries.

The doctor in Bangkok told me the best way to get better from this Salmonella poisoning is to stay at home or in hotel, taking it easy for two weeks and taking the sulpha drugs. As this is not possible with my itinerary, I must do the following: don't get too cold, so no swimming; or too hot, which is difficult when it's 36° celsius with high humidity; avoid spicy food as much as possible, which is difficult in this part of the world, especially as I like it; eat small meals often; drink lots of liquid, especially strong tea; no alcohol. Unfortunately this tour group like their drink, and I keep getting offered whiskies and beers, which I have to decline. This routine of do's and don'ts has to continue until the Salmonella is proved to have gone, by reporting to a convenient hospital a few days after I've finished the Sulpha course.

Being a fishing town there is a lot of fresh fish in the restaurants. The fish is on display, on ice outside the restaurant; you discuss the relative merits of different fish, make your choice, it's weighed, the price is given and you have it cooked exactly how you like. I usually have mine with fried mixed vegetables Thai style, with rice, similar to Chinese style.

I went for a walk to the local beach and was glad I wasn't swimming as there were many giant jelly fish washed up on the beach – one foot in diameter!

Night at Supamitr Hotel, Hua-Hin.

Day 95. Thursday March 18. Hua-Hin.

Today the group went on an organized trip by two mini-buses to Sam Roi Yot National Park – took a boat trip round rock islands and landed on a beach – had to take shoes off to get ashore from knee depth water – walked and climbed high to visit Tham Phraya Nakhorn cave – a long hard rocky climb – two ladies had to turn back as they had unsuitable footwear – definitely one of my 'don't do it' things, as it made me too hot! But then it was only supposed to be a short walk. It took 1¾ hours return trip and I was glad to be carrying a litre of water!

We had lunch in a beach cafe, then returned by the same boat, with the same wading out to the boat in order to board. This was an enjoyable visit, but we had no guide to tell us about the wild life in the National park, and Steve, our tour leader, told us nothing.

We had the use of two day rooms at the hotel as we were staying until 6.30 p.m. when we had to leave to catch the International Express night train at Hua-Hin station to Malaysia.

It's a very comfortable sleeper train with buffet for dinner and breakfast. There was much merriment in our group as some people had a little too much to drink.

Night Sleeper Train to Padang Besar, Malaysia.

Day 96. Friday March 19. Hua-Hin to Georgetown.

In the morning we arrived at the Malaysian border and had to change trains, also through immigration and customs – had to open my case for examination – the second time, having crossed 13 borders so far.

Arrived at Butterworth where we had quite a walk to the ferry across to Penang Island. Taxi to the hotel in the town of Georgetown. Penang Island is 13 kilometres in circumference.

In the afternoon I walked round town with Les and Linda, visiting the harbour and temples, and St. George's Anglican Church which we managed to get the verger to open specially for us. It is the oldest building in town, built in 1812. We ended up having a Chinese meal in the Hong Kong restaurant. On the way back we called in to an open air bar where we had coffee and listened to a group with girl singer.

The trains in Thailand and Malaysia are comfortable and air conditioned with reclining airline type seats. However, the safety of passengers is not of prime concern, as most of the outside doors are left open and swinging on their hinges. They are inside opening doors, so each time I go for a walk I close lots of them. Some just won't close as the locks are broken.

Night at Mingood Hotel, Georgetown, Penang.

Day 97. Saturday March 20. Georgetown.

I joined a group of 8 people on an optional tour round Penang Island, which is about 1 mile off the mainland. We hired two taxis and the tour included a Chinese Pagoda Temple, a butterfly farm which is very similar to the one in Syon Park in West London. The others had never seen such beautiful butterflies. We visited Penang Museum, then a reptile house with insects, mainly giant beetles and spiders, then a botanical garden, which also had a reptile house, also aviary. We ended up at a beach where some people swam. I didn't – No Swimming! although it was tempting in the heat and humidity of this place.

We returned to Georgetown by two local buses and at my suggestion decided to go to the top of a tower block of 65 floors called Komtar. I was fairly certain that such a building would have a visitors' gallery, although we had not seen any signs or publicity on the matter. (There seems to be a good tourist industry here in Malaysia, but they don't have leaflets on what to see and where to go, and maps etc.) The first five storeys of this building comprise a huge shopping complex, and it took us half an hour to find the place on the ground floor where the lift starts. The visitors' gallery is on the 58th floor with lots more shops. It cost $5 Malaysian (£1.40), but with the same ticket you could also buy goods to the value of $5 free! I bought biscuits and snacks in the food market, so it cost nothing really, to go to the top!

We finished the day with a meal in an Indian/Malaysian restaurant called Yasmeen, which was recommended in The Lonely Planet Guide. Cheap meal including 2 fruit juice drinks at less than £1 ($3.15 Malaysian).

Western type food is sometimes on menus in local restaurants, but it's never quite what you would expect, because they've got no idea what it's supposed to be like, e.g. pepper steak is just a hamburger with loads of pepper sprinkled on just before serving with fried vegetables. Chinese tea is cheap at £0.06 a cup, but a cup of what you might call ordinary English tea is £0.24, and comes with condensed milk very often. Coffee is a hit or miss affair because it is usually far too strong, and you get a saucerful as well.

Night at Mingood Hotel, Georgetown, Penang.

Day 98–99. Sunday–Monday March 21–22. Georgetown to Brinchang.

We left Mingood Hotel early at 6.30 a.m. by taxi to the

ferry port, our luggage went on a big trolley on to the ferry, then off the ferry and the long walk to Butterworth Station (I can't get used to these British place names here, also Cameron Highlands doesn't seem to ring true in the middle of South East Asia!) Caught the 7.30 train to Tapah Road for Cameron Highlands. This train goes through to Singapore daily, but we are doing two stopovers in Cameron Highlands and Kuala Lumpur.

The Cameron Highlands is 5000 ft above sea level and therefore cooler with less humidity, and hotels do not need air-conditioning for cooling. It's quite cool at night too, so you need covers on the bed, which is more comfortable. It's mainly jungle covering most of the area, including hill tops and valleys. You can hardly call these hills mountains because the tops are only 1000 ft above the valleys. However, apart from the golf course near the hotel, it's like I would have expected Malaysia to be – Jungle! There are a few villages, this one is called Brinchang. People come here to go walking in the jungle on marked trails. I went on a 4 km walk with 4 other people, it was a lot of rough climbing and scrambling, many ups and downs and quite strenuous. It was under forest canopy all the time and we never saw any sky, nor any wildlife except insects. There are supposed to be snakes, but we never saw any.

The village is quite small and can be explored in 30 minutes. There are lots of restaurants, and I ate twice in an Indian/Malaysian one. I have been eating vegetarian for a few days, just to avoid meat, as it's never served hot, and therefore always suspicious.

On arriving here, the journey from the station took two hours by taxi, and was climbing in low gear most of the way, with many hairpin bends, and for most people, including me, it was one of the most unpleasant car rides we'd ever had. Our tour leader Steve, and some other people were ill for the rest of the day, after we arrived mid-afternoon.

One afternoon five of us hired a taxi to tour the local attractions: a mushroom farm, a strawberry farm where this climate gives a continuous 12 months a year production, and after 2 or 3 years each plant is replaced, a tea plantation – a major industry here, a coffee plantation, a rose farm where most roses are produced and sold as flowers, but 16 acres are used solely for the cultivation of a very dark red rose, and the petals are used to make a thick concentrate of fruit juice and jam – we sampled this at a tasting session, finally a fruit market where we sampled tree tomatoes.

Two nights at Parklands Hotel, Brinchang.

Day 100. Tuesday March 23. Brinchang to Kuala Lumpur.

On leaving Brinchang this morning we all insisted the taxi drivers went slower and stopped for breaks, and we coped with the 2 hour journey of hairpin bends much better this time. We caught the 11.30 train to Kuala Lumpur, arriving hotel about 3.30 p.m.

I walked round town with some others in the boiling heat to change money and have a snack in a restaurant in Chinatown. In the evening I went out to take night photographs of the Sultan Abdul Sahmed building, a palace of moorish design which is lit up at night and is the most photographed building in town. I still don't know how good my night photography was in India as I haven't seen the results...still, I can only try!

Night at Grand Olympic Hotel, Kuala Lumpur.

Day 101. Wednesday March 24. Kuala Lumpur to Singapore.

I joined Mavis, Rae, and Les on a coach tour of the city. We arrived back late so there was no time for lunch before departure to Kuala Lumpur station at 2.30. Caught the 3 o'clock express to Singapore. Arrived hotel just before midnight and finished the day with coffee in the restaurant.

Night at Grand Central Hotel, Singapore.

Day 102. Thursday March 25. Singapore.

I toured the town with Les, and travelled on the new MRT (Mass Rapid Transit) underground system which has completely automatic trains and ticketing. I remember this being built in 1985, as was evidenced by all the massive holes for construction we noticed in the city. Also went to the refurbished Raffles Hotel to have a look at its new style, but didn't have a Singapore Sling! The hotel has been brought up to date, but doesn't have that nostalgic feeling about it, as I remembered from 1985. It is too modern with its posh, trendy shopping arcades all around the outside.

Visited the President's Palace Park and listened to a schools' brass band playing, which was very enjoyable. I had intended to go to the other end of Orchard Road to visit the Hotel I stayed at in 1985, but never got round to it. Orchard Road looks the same – full of shopping arcades, and very lively in the evening with musical groups playing.

Singapore is very hot, very humid, and very expensive, prices being much about the same as in England, I should think, using the benchmark of a McDonald's breakfast at $5 (Singapore), £2 (English), at the cheap end of the market. I have been used to such cheap food and goods generally throughout the Middle East and Asia. Since leaving India 5 weeks ago each country has been more expensive than the previous one, starting with Kathmandu in Nepal, then Thailand, then Malaysia, and Singapore. (I'm not sure about Indonesia yet, although I'm actually writing this in Djakarta, and being a little behind with my Journal!).

Night at Grand Central Hotel, Singapore.

Day 103. Friday March 26. Singapore.

Made a fairly early start today, having decided to get out of town for the day with three others, and took the bus and cable car to Sentosa Island. The Island is more commercialized than it was 8 years ago, and the most interesting feature, which I don't remember from before, is gardens with waterfalls and fountains, which go on and on up hill and down again for many hundreds of metres. There is a central main section of a large semi-circle of lake with fountains and waterfalls, surrounded by an ampitheatre with seats. Obviously this is for musical presentations etc. although it was empty of people at the time, but coming out of some hidden source – there must have been massive stereo loudspeakers – was the most nostalgic, moving music I have ever heard in such beautiful surroundings. It was music of the Pan Flutes, and it filled the air over the whole ampitheatre. I just stood transfixed and listened, then took a few photos of the area. I made a mental note that I must find out what the recording was so that I could get hold of a copy.

The cable car station for Sentosa is at the top of the World Trade Centre building, and it's a bit frightening when the cable car goes over the edge of the building and you suddenly find yourself looking straight down into the sea!

Trivia:
>Pewter: 97% tin, 3% copper and antimony.
>Martabak: A delicious Indian vegetable dish I ate in Malaysia. Layers of pancake and vegetable infill.
>Jim Thompson disappeared in the jungle in the Cameron Highlands in 1967. He was an American who revived the Thai silk industry after World War 2, and his house is now a museum in Bangkok. We went over it in 1985.
>Batik: Wax material printing technique.

Night at the Grand Central Hotel, Singapore.

Day 104. Saturday March 27. Singapore to Cirebon.

Departed hotel 9.30 a.m. for Singapore Changi Airport and flight to Djakarta, then bus to Djakarta rail station where we had 3 hours to spare before our train to Cirebon. Went to look at the National Monument in Merdeka (Independence) Square, 132 metres high and topped by a flame of pure gold. The lift to the top was unfortunately closed. I went back to the station and phoned Pat with two phone cards. We caught the 5.30 p.m. Cirebon train which arrived about 8 p.m. This is the final train journey on this trip to Bali, the rest of the trip being by bus and one more flight.

Immediately after checking in to the hotel I decided I must get some money changed, so I caught a bicycle rickshaw (a Becak), which is different from the Indian rickshaw in that the passenger sits in the front facing forward with the driver behind. It was pouring with rain, so for the very first time since leaving London, I had to wear my raincoat, but I still got very wet. I asked the driver to take me to the nearest money changer, but they had all closed so he took me to a shop that would do some unofficially. They opened specially for me so I changed £20 cash. The rate they first offered was very low, but I happened to have seen the newspaper official rate that day, so was able to bargain for a higher rate which was still lower than the official rate to be had from the money changers. However, I had no choice, as I needed the money – I had spent all my money phoning home unexpectedly from Djakarta, so I had a late dinner at the hotel, finishing at 12 midnight.

Night at Sidodadi Hotel, Cirebon.

Day 105. Sunday March 28. Cirebon.

Went on a tour with the group by mini-bus for the whole morning to Trusmi Batik village and the Sunyaragh Meditation Garden. We were supposed to see the batik artists at work in a factory, but it was unexpectedly closed. The meditation garden was unique in that it was a maze of caves, archways, walkways, and steps, all over this garden setting, all man-made with primitive looking bricks and stones. There were pools also, but the garden and pools had not been maintained recently due to lack of funds. It was a paradise for the local children who were playing Indonesian hide and seek (I think) in the caves and passage ways. There was a flat, covered, marble slab for the king to sit and meditate – the garden was about 400 years old.

In the afternoon I walked with Les and Lyndon the one kilometre to town and looked round a department store, also had lunch in the store cafeteria which was self-service. The menu was only in Indonesian, so we had difficulty sorting out what we wanted with the aid of a list of words in a guide book. We had Ayam Goreng (chicken with vegetables and noodles), plus clear soup with meat ball sausages, also Fanta drink. The meal was more than I really wanted, for the price of 80 pence each! Local food is cheap because they don't cater for tourists, hence no English on the menu. I didn't see any tourists at all.

I was sure I had left my hat on the cashier's desk while sorting out the money. When I went back I was unable to explain to the cashier girl my loss, in spite of my charade for 'loss of a hat'. I wished I had my Japanese friend with me (he had partial hearing) from the Cairo to Kathmandu trip, because he could explain anything to anyone without words, and very descriptive too! I went back to the others to think! I then had the idea to look among the people in the restaurant for someone with a hat on, which might make it easier to explain. I finally found a young man wearing a hat and managed to get him to understand my charade, with the help of his hat and his friends, and much laughter. No one understood a word of English. He came over to the cashier and explained my problem. She had my hat under her desk all the time. So much for my charade!

I have got lazy and don't make enough effort to learn some words in the local language, or even get a phrase book. I started this trip with all good intentions, and made the effort until Turkey, which was the 7th country, where I just gave up, the effort was too much.

Whilst doing my charade to the cashier girl, there was a queue of locals waiting with their food trays to pay their bills, watching this crazy foreigner doing some kind of a comedy act! But there was no problem with their meals getting cold while they waited for me to finish, because they don't understand the concept of 'hot meals' in this part of the world. Most meals which you would expect to be hot are either only warm or cold. The exceptions are in some better class hotels where some meals are served hot. In

Kathmandu, which is packed with westerners, the catering community have got the message, during the last twenty years, of the strange western habit of having hot meals.

There is a conflict of choice here in Asia, on the matter of where to eat because of lack of hygiene in kitchens, and in the handling and storage of food. I have thought a lot about this because somewhere along my route, in Pakistan, India or Nepal I contracted Salmonella poisoning.

On the one hand you have the restaurants cooking for lots of people at any one time and therefore there is a waiting time between cooking and serving – unless the staff make an effort to reduce this waiting time, the food will often be only warm, and most places don't make the effort because they don't understand the western habit of hot meals. The more up market you go the more the staff understand the western habit. And who knows, when the meat or chicken is only warm, whether it was cooked properly in the first place. You can't see the kitchen in these places!

On the other hand, you have the food stalls where they set up shop on the pavement with a kerosene burner, a few cooking bowls, a bench seat and a wooden table, and with a bit of imagination could be called a cafe. You really see life in these places, with traffic racing past a few feet away. Sometimes, in the better ones, there is a piece of cloth hanging down over the roof edge so that you don't actually see the traffic! But here you can see what's going on, you sit and watch the routine of food preparation. It's better if they are cooking for another customer as you can watch before ordering, see where the chicken comes from, is it in a plastic container? (not very often) or covered in flies?– do they cook it enough? On the few occasions I've eaten in such places, a good bet is to have fried noodles or rice, with vegetables and egg, and you see them frying it all up. You can make them boil it up more by a descriptive action with the hands (learnt from Sato my Japanese friend). So there is something to be said for such places. Sometimes a chicken is cooked on a spit and looks very appetizing sizzling away.

Another hygiene problem is cutlery: is it washed

properly? in what sort of second hand water? or dried on a dirty cloth? There is just the same problem in proper restaurants where you can't see the kitchen. I've eaten a few times in places in India, Nepal and Malaysia where you're expected to eat with your hand (Right hand only! Left hand is reckoned to be unclean for unmentionable reasons). There is always a water tap somewhere to wash hands even if it's right out on the edge of the road. Rice is difficult! But we have been taught to squeeze it into a pyramid shape in order to pick up a suitable amount. The ultimate in hygienic cleanliness is a place where food is served on banana leaves and eaten with washed hands, then the remains, including the banana leaves, are scooped up at the end and thrown away. No washing up! Low overheads! I've had hot vegetable samosas served on a neatly made inverted pyramid shaped piece of leaf which you just throw away after use – the best of bio-degradable eating plates.

Night at Sidodadi Hotel, Cirebon.

Day 106. Monday March 29. Cirebon to Yogjakarta.

We departed Cirebon at noon by coach to Yogjakarta, a 7 hour journey. All the coaches and trains we travel in are comfortable and air-conditioned.

The first job to be done here in Yogjakarta is to go to the emergency department of a local hospital to get myself checked for Salmonella, as it's 3 days since I finished the Sulpha drug course. I managed to coerce Ruth, a friend in our group, who happens to be a Senior Staff Nurse at Harefield Hospital, to come with me. I thought she would be interested in the workings of a third world hospital, and anyway, I felt better being with someone. We went to the Muslim hospital, which was recommended, and after registration was seen immediately by a lady doctor. She and the nurses were very nice, clean and polite, and looked much like the staff in an English hospital, with doctor wearing a long white coat, and stethoscope sticking out of pocket. The laboratory, where we waited for blood test results, was open to the elements i.e. no glass in window spaces, and not very clean. Nevertheless all were going about their business, and seemed to know what they were doing. The hospital was not up to the same standard as the one in Bangkok, which was of a standard one would expect in Europe..

Result of my test was positive – disappointing! Salmonella blood count was 400:1 whereas maximum safety level was 200:1, so I have to take sulpha drugs for another week and report for further tests in Bali or Cairns or Sydney. But I feel fine..! I had late dinner with Ruth, Stephanie, Lyndon, and Chris, it was Indonesian and therefore cheap.

This Kirana Guest House is a beautiful place with ground level rooms, with settee, chairs and table on our own private patio looking out over the gardens. The hotel won the best hotel garden award for 1991.

Night at Kirana Guest House, Yogjakarta.

Day 107. Tuesday March 30. Yogjakarta.

Yogjakarta is a Batik centre in Java, so I went with six others to a whole day Batik course where I made a 6 colour design suitable for framing, or maybe a cushion cover. Also I bought a professionally made Batik art piece so that I can show the comparison of the two back home. Bought also a set of artists' tools with artist daughter Claire in mind who might be interested to experiment, under my expert supervision!

In the evening went with the group to the Yogjakarta Ballet performance in an open air theatre. We all went on Bekacs and got there early to have a conducted tour of the performers' dressing rooms while they were preparing for the show. We took photographs of them made up in their 'war paint'. The theme of the show was legendary, but the ballet was excellent, culminating with the heroine being burned alive in a real semi-circle of fire. Took some photographs at the end when we mingled with some of the dancers who were Steve's friends. Steve, our tour leader, has done this overland trip 18 times and therefore has got to know some of the people connected with the individual trips and shows we see.

Night at Kirana Guest House, Yogjakarta.

Day 108. Wednesday March 31. Yogjakarta.

The rickshaw cycles for two people are called Bekacs and passengers face forward as described before at Cirebon stopover. I shared a Bekac today with Linda, my American friend. The cost including driver was 1000 Rupees (£1) for the day. Did shopping, clothes and art. Missed the King's Palace which closed too early at noon. Visited the bird market, and bats. Saw shadow puppet show Agastya which had Indonesian orchestral accompaniment, but the performance was so steeped in Javanese and religious culture that it was impossible to understand in spite of a write-up in English. The poem portayed was 'the longest poem in the world' according to the write-up, and it seemed like it too! I came out half way through – most unlike me! The puppets move so slowly and infrequently that it gets boring, although we could sit either side of the screen, sometimes to watch the orchestra playing their drum-like instruments.

Our Bekac driver heard us talking about what to do for lunch, so he recommended somewhere nearby which turned out to be a pavement cafe with a wooden table and bench seat, with kerosene burner and a few cooking bowls. A chicken was sticking out of a cooking bowl and others were hanging down from hooks. With some trepidation we ordered fried chicken, noodles and vegetables, but then we saw the chicken being cut for another customer with flies all over it. We changed our minds and had fried noodles, with egg and vegetables all mixed up together, which we had seen cooking for another customer, bubbling up quite a lot, and it seemed, and was, all right.

Tea in Indonesia is served in large glasses (half litre), hot or cold, no milk, and with 3 heaped dessert spoonfuls of sugar, unless you say you want no sugar. So their tea is like tea flavoured sugar syrup!

In the evening I celebrated my wedding anniversary with Les, Linda, Mavis, and Rae, we drank whiskies and rum. Later I phoned home to Pat to wish her a happy anniversary.

Night at Kirana Guest House, Yogjakarta.

Days 109-110. Thursday-Friday April 1-2. Yogjakarta to Bandungan.

We had an early breakfast followed by departure by coach to Bandungen, stopping cn route at Borobodur, a Buddhist stupa, which is the oldest and largest Buddhist monument in the southern hemisphere built around 8th/9th century. There are two million blocks of stone to the circular structure which has 9 terraces – 6 squares and 3 circles – each of decreasing size, and each one having a walkway round the edge with steps up to the next one. Each terrace represents a different stage on the way to spiritual perfection, the upper level being Nirvana. There are 1460 individual panels depicting scenes from Buddhist mythology on the galleries, and 500 life size Buddha statues, some now headless. For 9 centuries, when Buddhist kingdoms shifted to East Java, the structure was allowed to decay and collapse, and was partly buried by volcanic eruptions. However, in 1814, during the British occupation, a Mr. Raffles re-discovered it completely covered in vegetation and rubble, with stones scattered everywhere. A massive clean up operation commenced, but it was inadequate.

In 1907 the Dutch government did a restoration lasting 5 years supervised by Van Erp, an army engineer. But still the basic problems were not solved of shifting foundations and internal decay through inadequate drainage. The only solution would be a complete re-construction. The Indonesian government went to UNESCO in 1973 who collected donations internationally and finally got the 22 Million $US to finance the job. Each of the 2 million stones was dismantled and numbered, new foundations and drainage laid, and the whole thing re-built with stone replacements where necessary. It was completed in 1983 after 10 years. Quite a feat! Like Abu Simbel in Egypt.

Arrived in Bandungan for a late lunch. Hotel was all two storey apartments with 3 bedrooms and shared facilities and living rooms, all set in old Java style gardens, with tennis courts, swimming pool and aviaries. Also individually caged birds that woke everyone at 5 a.m. with their "Cock-a doodle-oo-oo." Some cages were inconsiderately sited next to the front doors of the apartments, including mine, so that you had a one time only 'bird alarm' set at dawn!

Our apartment had lounge with T.V. and kitchen for self-catering – not that we self-catered, but we could make tea, coffee easily. There were 4 others in my flat. The first morning I and two others wanted to go to the local flower and vegetable market – early morning – so I set the alarm for 5.15. I needn't have bothered, as the 'bird alarm' went off at 5 a.m. We made coffee and watched early morning martial arts type aerobics on T.V. and I left for the market at 5.45 with my two lady companions, the other two flat mates didn't want to come. These two ladies were dancers from the Yogjakarta Ballet show we saw two nights ago, so perhaps need a bit of explaining as to why they were sharing my flat. They were friends of Steve, our tour leader, who has made friends with many people connected with all the events and travelling done during the 18 times he has led this tour for Trailfinders. He gets discounted rates for his groups and also recommends other tour operators to these cultural events, coach tours, hotels, travel agents etc., so all concerned get more business and it helps everyone – that's the way it works everywhere. These two were lead dancers in the ballet and every two months, so I gather, were invited to the next stopover with the group for a two day break with free accommodation and breakfast – a short holiday between ballet performances.

Bandungan is a hill resort with very pleasant climate where air conditioning is not needed in hotels, and our group was allocated a liberal amount of accommodation, more than was actually needed, in these self-contained apartments, hence the two extra people made no difference to the hotel. They just happened to be allocated the same flat as me. Lucky me! I took lots of photographs at the flower market and fruit market, and they enjoyed playing the role of 'westerners' with western type clothes and a camera – like tourists. I expect they meet a lot of westerners and are probably envious of our way of life. They bought lots of fruit for their families, because it was cheaper than in Yogjakarta. We returned for breakfast at 8 o'clock. They were to return later in the morning to be in time for the next ballet performance that evening.

After breakfast I ordered a taxi for Les and me, to go to Gedong Songo – which means 'nine temples' – six kilometres away. Each temple is set on its own hill, and they are all scattered over the slopes of Mount Ungaran; all are 8th/9th century. We walked round a set route of 3 kilometres which took 2 hours, very scenic and scrambling terrain, including hot sulphur springs. The temples are *Shivaite Hindu*, and are said to be set in the most beautiful temple site in Java. From the topmost temple can be seen the surrounding volcanoes. There was no organized trip to climb to the rim of Mount Merapi, the most volatile of the volcanoes, as I thought there would be.

It rained for most of the afternoon and evening, so I didn't do much except make coffee, write, and watch T.V. We had dinner in the hotel.

Two nights at Rawa Pening Hotel, Bandungan.

Day 111. Saturday April 3. Bandungan to Bali.

Departed Bandungan 8 a.m. for 3 hour coach ride to Yogjakarta airport, then a 1½ hour flight to Denpasar, Bali by Garuda Airlines. The lunch snack on board was typical Indonesian food – meat cake, and firm custardy pudding – most people didn't attempt to eat it, but it was only a local flight by an Indonesian airline so we couldn't expect western food. Later, on the international flight Bali to Cairns, the food was excellent by western standards, this was also Garuda Airlines. Arrived hotel early evening.

We had a farewell dinner at the hotel restaurant, an excellent buffet of Western or Indonesian style which was half paid for by Steve as part of the tour package. So we all paid 5000 Rupiahs (£1.70) each. The group collected 160,000 Rupiahs as a gift to Steve, our tour leader.

I phoned the airport to check Pat's flight arrival tomorrow, they said there was no KLM flight Sunday, the next incoming KLM flight was Monday – there was no doubt! They were sure! The KLM office was closed as it was the week-end, so I couldn't ask them. Either I had misunderstood Pat on the phone, or the flight was changed!

On consulting with Steve I decided it could well be a case of typical Asian misinformation, written about before in this journal. You just can't believe what they tell you – check it again and again. But there was no one else to check with, so I decided to wait until the morning, and check again when a different shift would be on duty at the airport flight information desk.

Night at Puri Klapa Garden Cottages, Sanur, Bali.

Day 112. Sunday April 4. Bali.

Sure enough this morning, they said there was an incoming KLM flight at 15.00, which is what it should be, so I decided to believe it as it was the answer I wanted.

I walked to Sanur Beach Hotel to check reservations that Pat and I had previously booked, cancelled tonight's reservation, then back at Puri Klapa Cottages I arranged for Pat to stay with me tonight, so we could be with the group for the last day. The tour was, unknown to me before I met with the group in Bangkok, extended one extra day, which is today Sunday, hence the need for me to change hotel bookings.

I met Pat at the airport on time, and we had lots to talk about, news about our new grand daughter Heather, my mother's funeral, and how Michael (our son) and Diane (his girl friend) were getting along in Australia, where we were due to meet up in two weeks' time. Later, we had dinner out with Mavis, Rae, and Les.

Night at Puri Klapa Garden Cottages, Sanur, Bali.

Stage 5
Bali to Los Angeles

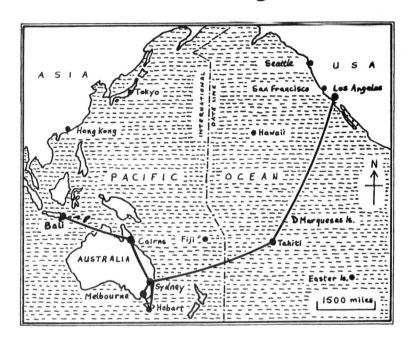

Pat joins me on this section, where, after a few days in Bali, we fly to Australia, staying at Cairns, Sydney, Canberra, and Melbourne. We then fly to Tasmania, and spend a week touring and visiting a relative, and fly back to Sydney. Here we spend a week with Michael, and Diane his girl friend. We then fly to Tahiti for a few days stopover, before flying on to Los Angeles. Here I carry on with my round the world trip while Pat flies back home to London. Distance 13,050 miles, 30 days.

Day 113. Monday April 5. Bali.

The Puri Klapa Garden Cottages are in a lovely setting of simulated jungle, and there is a good swimming pool where we spent some time before saying goodbye to the few remaining members of the group. We then checked out at 12 noon, and went by taxi to the Sanur Beach Hotel, which was palatial, with cafe and restaurant prices to match the splendour of the place. We relaxed around the swimming pool and beach area, which was very enjoyable as the weather was hot at 34°c and very humid.

Met Mavis, Rae, and Les for dinner at the 'Swastika One' restaurant. Eating out is still cheap compared to England – just over £3 each for dinner including beer beforehand – but for me Bali was just a bit more expensive than Java, which was more expensive than Malaysia, and so on back to India, where prices were so low. We expect prices in Australia to be similar to England.

Night at Sanur Beach Hotel, Bali.

Day 114. Tuesday April 6. Bali.

Left hotel before breakfast at 7.30 to go to Besakih Temple by public bus and bemos (these are mini-buses which run on a very casual basis and are not scheduled like a public bus). However, both need negotiating for fare. Drivers always ask a high fare for tourists, so it's a question of bargaining for a fair price. It took 5 buses or bemos going, and only 4 coming back as we stopped at a dance theatre on the way. The journey was Sanur to Denpasar, Batubulan, Batubulan Dance Theatre, Klungkung, Besakih. The cultural dance show was Barong and Kriss, and was excellent. The hassle in travelling the above buses was wearing, but worth the local colour of the locals getting on and off the bus. I introduced Pat to a roadside stall cafe where we had coffee.

It was festival time in Bali and all the streets were decorated and many people were going to temples with their offerings: flowers, rice, spices, often in small baskets or in banana leaf dishes. Besakih Mother Temple was beautifully decorated, and we took some colourful photographs. Returned to hotel about 5 o'clock and had a swim in the pool. We had dinner in the restaurant opposite hotel drive – The Balita.

Night at Sanur Beach Hotel, Bali.

Day 115. Wednesday April 7. Bali.

We are eating all our meals in the above mentioned 'Belita' restaurant, as the food is good value for money. Spent the morning at leisure on the beach and in hotel swimming pool. In the afternoon we went on an organized mini-bus tour with guide to Mengwi State Temple of the Royal Mengwi Dynasty; Alas Kedaton, the holy forest where tame monkeys take food out of your hand; Tanah Lot, a spectacular sea temple where we were supposed to see the sunset, but as it was cloudy we took a few photographs and returned early before sunset.

Night at Sanur Beach Hotel, Bali.

Day 116. Thursday April 8. Bali.

We went swimming in pool and sea and stayed in the area all morning. Checked out of hotel at noon and left cases with the porter until 9 p.m. I bought a Batik shirt and we spent the rest of the afternoon around pool and sea area. Had dinner in our usual restaurant where I was presented with a gift from the manager for my birthday – a fan to keep me cool.

At 9 o'clock we took a taxi to Denpasar Airport for our overnight flight to Cairns by Garuda, the Indonesian airline. Breakfast on the plane was excellent.

Overnight flight to Cairns.

Day 117. Friday April 9. Cairns.

We arrived early morning and were met at airport by limousine service for trip to hotel. The hotel is colonial style with 'open to air' public rooms, as climate seems to be tropical, with single storey rooms set in tropical gardens, including two rock and landscaped swimming pools. Pat and I went to town in morning by courtesy hotel bus service and walked round promenade area by sea. Buffet dinner in hotel.

Night at Cairns Colonial Club, Cairns.

93

Day 118. Saturday April 10. Cairns.

We were picked up early by Quicksilver Tours for the trip to Agincourt platform on the barrier reef, which is 26 nautical miles out from Port Douglas. It was a super sparkling silver boat 'Catamaran VII' which cruised at about 26 knots. The wind was blowing at 20 knots so it was a very rough passage and we all took sea sickness tablets. Nevertheless, lots of people were ill.

Went on a semi-submersible boat with under water viewing and went swimming in the fairly rough sea, depth about 10 metres. Also went down to an under water section of the platform for viewing and taking photos. We were well provided with food and drink, with coffee before starting, an excellent prawn and meat buffet served during the 3 hours on the platform, and afternoon tea before leaving the platform. Weather was sunny and very windy with a big swell running, making the ride very uncomfortable.

Night at Cairns Colonial Club, Cairns.

Day 119. Sunday April 11. Cairns.

We were picked up at the hotel by an Australian Pacific coach and taken to Kuranda where we spent 5 hours walking round village markets and going to an aboriginal Tjapukai Dance Theatre where a thoroughly modern show was put on. It rained a lot of the time, so we were constantly dodging showers. We had lunch, then a beer in a local pub. As part of the tour we travelled back on the Kuranda Tourist Train, which was a spectacular 1½ hour journey down from the village in the mountains back to Cairns.

Night at Cairns Colonial Club, Cairns.

Day 120. Monday April 12. Cairns to Sydney.

Picked up by a limousine service for transfer to airport at 11 a.m. and flight to Sydney by Australian Airlines. Good lunch on plane and arrived at hotel at 5 o'clock. Our first impression of Sydney was of a rude taxi driver who objected to helping with cases at the airport and on arrival at the hotel. He just pressed the 'boot open' button and said, "The boot's open," and stayed in his seat!

The 'Kendall' is a restored pair of Victorian terraced houses with extension at back, with a garden terrace where we had breakfast and 24 hour tea or coffee, also a Jacuzzi. The area is called Kings Cross which is a bit run down to what it used to be in Victorian times. The road is called Victoria Street. In the tourist brochure it is called 'Bed and Breakfast – Provides Victorian Comforts', but it is far better than you would expect a 'B & B' to be in England.

The first thing I had to do in Sydney was to find the local hospital and get my test done for Salmonella. We found St.Vincent's Hospital and I was seen fairly quickly in Emergency. The doctor was alarmed when I told her that the doctor in Bangkok had said I had a form of typhoid, as this is a notifiable disease! They could not get the results of my test for 48 hours, when I will have left Sydney, so I will have to come back in 12 days time when I'm next in Sydney. I had to strip and put hospital gown on, and had many tests done, but not a blood test, as this would only show the body's reaction to Salmonella or that I was a carrier, neither of which would mean that I had the disease! The hospital in Indonesia, the doctor said, was wrong in giving me a blood test only, to prove I had or had not the disease. The only sure test was a stool test. After much consultation with her colleagues and textbooks, she assured me I did not and could not have any form of Salmonella which was related to typhoid itself. I was to come back in 12 days time to get the test result and take it from there! Anyway, I still feel fine, and am beginning to wonder what all the fuss is about!

I happened to be in bed when the dinner trolley came round, so I had a free dinner, also I was not charged any fee! So far..! Pat waited outside for me all this time – 1½ hours. Afterwards, we walked round the town, and to the Circular Quay at the harbour, then came back by underground train.

Night at The Kendall, Sydney.

Day 121. Tuesday April 13. Sydney.

We bought a 'Hopper' one–day underground ticket and saw the sights: the Harbour, Bridge, Darling Harbour and the Opera House, where we bought tickets for a performance in 2 weeks time. In the evening we had a Chinese meal in Chinatown.

Night at The Kendall, Sydney.

Day 122. Wednesday April 14. Sydney to Canberra.

We took an early (7.30 a.m.) taxi to the harbour coach terminal to join A.A.T.Kings 3 day tour to Melbourne. The coach was full with 50 people on board. We travelled south to Canberra where we had a city tour before being taken to the hotel.

Canberra is unusual in that it is a purpose built city started in 1927. It's very clean and beautiful with all the buildings fitting into a plan, whereas all other cities I know have been added to over centuries which, of course, is unavoidable. A particular feature is a suburb with many trees and landscaping, specifically for all the foreign embassies and consulates. All these are buildings of distinction.

The new Parliament House is a magnificent building with marble and wood interior. This contains the House of Representatives (like our House of Commons), and the Senate (like our House of Lords). All rooms and halls, except cabinet rooms and members' lobbies, were open to the public during the times when the M.P.'s were in session, plus normal office hours. The House of Reps. and the Senate were identical in shape, size, and seating, differing only in colour – olive green and china clay respectively. The public galleries were very comfortable, and the building was set in beautiful grounds and gardens

We enjoyed a barbecue lunch with wine at a nearby sheep station, with demonstrations of sheep shearing and boomerang throwing. We all had throws with varying degrees of accuracy. In the evening we had a champagne dinner at the hotel.

Night at Canberra Rex Hotel, Canberra.

Day 123. Thursday April 15. Canberra to Beechworth.

Had an early breakfast and left at 7.45 travelling to Cooma, the gateway to the snowy mountains – passed Jindabyne Dam and entered Kosciusko National Park where the mountain with the same name is the highest in Australia – 2228 metres. Continued to Thredbo village which is a ski resort in winter where we had lunch and walked alongside a river. Then on to Beechworth, arriving about 7 o'clock in the dark, at a motel. We also stopped and had a walk round Cooma, and Carryong.

Night at Carriage Motor Inn, Beechworth.

Day 124. Friday April 16. Beechworth to Melbourne.

I walked round Beechworth before breakfast, one of Australia's early gold mining towns with all wooden fronts to the shops.

Stopped at Bright for morning coffee, then on to Glenrowan where a Ned Kelly lived. He is a legendary figure who was forced into being a Bushranger (highwayman), by being accused of crimes he did not commit. There are some shops, and a museum dedicated to him; the village is a stop for all tourists. Had lunch in the Mangalore Pub. in Mangalore, then on to Chateau Tahbilk for a tour of the winery and cellars before wine tasting. We were taken on a cruise on the River Goulburn for 40 minutes, looking for wildlife – saw some birds. After disembarking, we had more wine tasting at Mitchelton Winery.

The tour concluded in Melbourne where we were dropped at the tour hotel (some people were continuing with a longer trip to Adelaide), where we took a taxi to our Motel which was just outside the centre of town, but within easy walking distance of the city centre.

Night at Downtown Motel, Melbourne.

Day 125. Saturday April 17. Melbourne.

Melbourne is a very modern city with many shopping plazas in large buildings of extra-ordinary design. Melbourne Central was such a one built like an inverted cone (point uppermost), and inside was a renovated listed building – a Shot Tower – where lead shot was dropped from a height to form a perfect sphere.

Most of today we walked along the river embankment and explored the most extensive Botanical Gardens.

Night at Downtown Motel, Melbourne.

Day 126. Sunday April 18. Melbourne to Launceston.

Looked round morning market before taking taxi to airport for flight to Launceston, Tasmania. The flight took 45 minutes during which time we managed to have soft drinks and a very substantial lunch.

Arrived at our motel about 3 p.m. having caught an airport bus service which was stopping at all hotels and motels.

One of the reasons why Pat and I have come to Launceston is so that we can look up a distant relative of mine – a Ken Bonney – who is a direct descendant of a convict who was transported to Australia in the early 1800's. We had corresponded as we were both interested in our family history, but my last letter to him had been returned as he had moved. Immediately on arrival I started phoning the K.Bonneys in the phone book, which turned out to be unsuccessful. Finally we called at his old address, and a neighbour told us the street where he lived, and that he collected old cars! We knocked on the door of a house that sported an old Austin Westminster 110, and that happened to be his house. We spent a pleasant couple of hours talking family history. He proved to be very knowledgeable about our common ancestry and had masses of information about the Bonney family, with a family tree propped up on his desk and numerous old photographs decorating the walls.

Pat and I had a good Pub. meal in the evening.

Night at Balmoral Motor Inn, Launceston, Tasmania.

A donkey trail viewed from the train, near Aswan.

Tea break at the 33–Arch Bridge, Esfahan.

Carol buying diesel fuel in
a filling station,
Baluchistan Desert.

Boarding a Rocket Bus,
Pakistan.

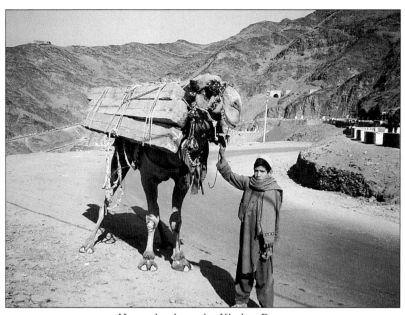

Heavy load, on the Khyber Pass.

In the grounds of Delhi Fort, making ends meet!

One of the beautiful
Indian dancers,
Jodhpur hotel.

Typical Indian village,
with Sato, Jodhpur.

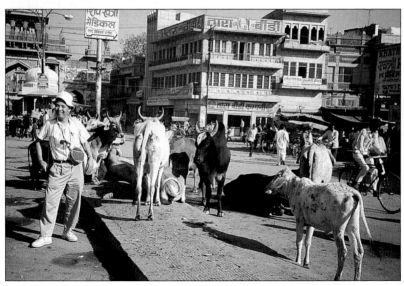

This family invited us to tea in their home, Jodhpur.

Early morning flower market in Bandungan, Java.

Besakih Mother Temple offerings, Bali.

Mengwi State Temple pagodas, with Pat, Bali.

Twilight reflections in Hobart Harbour, Tasmania.

Unusual Bronze Joggers in Riverside Park, Spokane, USA.

Typical Alaskan scenery from the train, Denali to Fairbanks.

The author at Niagara Falls.

Day 127. Monday April 19. Launceston.

Caught the 9.30 bus to Deloraine to look up more Bonneys about whom Ken had told us yesterday. The Bonneys were prominent farmers in the Deloraine district from the 1830's. John Bonney, the son of convict Joseph, originally bought the farm and it is now run by his descendant Jim whom we were not able to meet because he was out on the farm. However we met his elderly mother at her Home for the Aged and had an interesting chat with her. These Bonneys were most likely related to me by common ancestry, but I haven't yet proved it.

We visited St. Mark's Church and graveyard to photograph John Bonney's grave and commemorative plaque in the church. In Deloraine there was a Bonney's Inn, Bonney's Farm, and Bonney Play Group in the Baptist Church in Bonney Street. We liked Deloraine – a very small town. The lady in the tourist office was very helpful and knew everyone including the Bonney families.

After our dinner back in Launceston there was a message at the hotel that Ken Bonney had tried to contact us. We phoned and invited him to the hotel. He had found a photo of his ancestor John that he wanted to give to us. We spent a pleasant hour chatting over coffee. He was unmarried and we wondered to whom he would pass on the results of a vast amount of family history research he had done.

Night at Balmoral Motor Inn, Launceston.

Day 128. Tuesday April 20. Launceston.

We checked out of the Balmoral at 9.45 a.m. and the manager gave us a lift to the Launceston Novotel, a flashy up-market hotel. Pat and I went out for the rest of the morning – exploring the town and river bank – looking up lots of information held in the local library on the Bonney family. We got back into the hotel in time for a picnic lunch and met with the 'Royal Tasman' tour group at 1 o'clock for an afternoon tour. This was to Entally House, which is maintained for the National Trust at Hapsden, and is an early settlers' home – originally of a teenage girl convict who disguised herself as a boy.

Visited Cataract Gorge where we walked on a gorge trail for 1 hour. In the evening back at the hotel we were invited to a cocktail party by Australian Pacific, the operator of our tour. Later, at the hotel, we had a sumptuous buffet with many cooked meats, salads, cheeses, desserts and fruits.

Night at Launceston Novotel, Tasmania.

Day 129. Wednesday April 21. Launceston to Swansea.

We had an early breakfast and departed Launceston at 7.45 following the banks of the Tamar River to a small village modelled on the Swiss village of Grindelwald. This was built by a supermarket owner named Voss and was his dream village which he always wanted to build in Tasmania. Now the local laws are such that only Swiss style chalet houses are allowed to be built and the road layouts must conform to the original plans as laid down by Voss.

We passed over Batman bridge to Georgetown in the north. Then on to Scottsdale for lunch. A lot of the scenery here in Tasmania is just like it is in England as the climate is similar. Then on to Bickero to a wildlife park which we toured in a small train-like vehicle and saw pelicans and masses of ducks, all of which are fed by keepers. Toured an aviary and stroked a Tasmanian Devil (a beaver-type marsupial). Then to a restored mill which, years ago, used to mill bark from the Wattle tree, which in turn was used for tanning leather. This was near Swansea where our hotel was just about 30 yards from the beach.

Night at Swansea Inn, Swansea, Tasmania.

Day 130. Thursday April 22. Swansea to Port Arthur.

Had an early breakfast and left by coach at 7.45 for Ross, a historic town, and took photos of a bridge built by two stonemason convicts Daniel Herbert and James Colbeck. Daniel received a pardon for his work and carved his own memorial which marks his grave in the old burial ground. The bridge opened in 1836. The crossroads at the town centre has a building on each of its four corners which represent:

1. Temptation – The Man o' Ross Hotel.
2. Salvation – The Roman Catholic Church.
3. Recreation – The Town Hall, which accounted for much of the township's pleasures.
4. Damnation – The local gaol which incorporates the police station.

Then on to Richmond with a famous bridge built in the early 1820's. Here in Richmond we located the grave of Frances Atkins Bonney who died 1840, the wife of Joseph Bonney the convict. Ken Bonney had given us directions on where this was to be found in the St.Luke's Church Cemetery. We had a picnic lunch by the river, and then joined the group for the afternoon drive to Eaglehawk Neck, famous for its rugged coastal scenery. Here we visited four geological wonders: Tesselated Pavement, Blowhole, Devil's Kitchen and Tasman's Arch.

Visited Doo village where all house names contain 'Doo' i.e. Can-doo, Didgeridoo etc. Our motel overlooks the ruins of Port Arthur Penal Settlement. Saw a film archive in a special video showing for our group of 'For the Term of his Natural Life,' a film based on a convict story of Port Arthur made in 1927 – a silent film with sub-titles.

Night at Port Arthur Motor Inn, Tasmania.

Day 131. Friday April 23. Port Arthur to Hobart.

Had a fascinating tour of the Port Arthur Penal Colony which was operational from 1830-1877. The local guide brought the history of the place to life, and gave us all a very animated history lesson about the social problems in settling convicts and free people (soldiers and families), also the social problems in England that prompted the decision to send convicts to the other side of the world to Van Diemen's Land (Tasmania). Afterwards we went to an island called Isle of the Dead which was the burial ground for both prisoners and free people. This was a 1 hour trip in a cruise boat.

We all had lunch at the Bush Mill where we also saw a timber mill reconstruction of the last century with many working sections – all laid out like a museum with wooden houses typical of the period, also with realistic sound effects.

The tour ended at the Westside Hotel where we checked in and officially left the group. Later Pat and I explored Hobart town and harbour for 3½ hours and had a fish and chips take-away on a harbour bench seat. The weather was mild and warm at 25°c, the warmest for this time of year for 50 years, so they were saying on the news. Took a 'bulb' time photo of the harbour.

Night at Westside Hotel, Hobart.

Day 132. Saturday April 24. Hobart to Sydney.

We ordered an early airport bus to call at the hotel for 5.15 a.m. in order to catch the 7.10 a.m. flight to Sydney. The flight went like clockwork except that the first ten minutes was very rough and bumpy, like a bus going over bumps in the road, and was a bit frightening. At Sydney we also caught an airport bus to the hotel – it was cheap, and we had had enough of rude Australian taxi drivers! I have already mentioned the Sydney incident in this journal, and at Melbourne we only wanted to go about 3 blocks from the hotel we had been dropped at, to the motel where we were actually staying. The taxi driver reluctantly accepted our custom but he quite obviously didn't want a fare that was only $4.20 and he made his annoyance quite plain. As far as we are concerned Australian taxi drivers are rude, whereas the bus drivers are extremely pleasant.

At the hotel there were messages from our son Michael and friend Diane, also from a friend Don Riddle whom we hoped to see while in Sydney.

Very soon after arriving we left for the hospital to get the results of my Salmonella tests done two weeks ago. Had to wait a long time and it all took 2½ hours after reporting to the Emergency Casualty Department because they were so busy. Result is that I am clear of Salmonella (Hurrah!) but I have another bug called Campylobacter (a bacteria), which was unimportant as I had no adverse symptoms and therefore would be best left untreated. The doctor said if I was worried about it to see my G.P. on return to England – but I feel fine!

Pat and I eventually met up with Michael and Diane in the afternoon, and talked and looked at their photos while strolling round The Rock. We had dinner with them also.

Night at The Kendall, Sydney.

Day 133. Sunday April 25. Sydney.

Spent the day with Mike and Diane. We all have a 7–day bus/train/ferry pass and have used it quite a lot. We walked over the Sydney Harbour Bridge and climbed to the top to get a birds' eye view of the harbour, city and opera house and to take photographs. We did not do this as spidermen, there was a stairway of course! Also saw an exhibition and film of its construction between 1924-1932 – a marvellous feat of engineering and still the longest Arch Span Bridge in the world – British of course! Dorman Long of Middlesborough won the contract. Before this we had gone to Bondi Beach but the weather turned cold and rainy, so we did the bridge trip.

Afterwards we took a ferry to Watsons Bay and bus back, then on again to Bondi Beach where we had earlier seen a take–away fish and chip shop where they cook to order. We had a picnic on the beach by which time the weather had become mild and warmer. Bus and train back again. Mike and Diane are staying about 80 yards from our hotel in a backpackers' hostel.

Night at The Kendall, Sydney.

Day 134. Monday April 26. Sydney.

Today we went to look at the maritime museum, but it didn't have much about Botany Bay settlements, which is what we were particularly interested in, so we didn't go in. Took ferry to Circular Quay and made enquiries about visiting Botany Bay Visitor Centre, but it proved to be an impractical idea unless we hired a car. Met Mike and Diane at noon and decided to catch a ferry and bus to Balmoral Beach for swimming as it was a sunny day, and we did just that. But it was cold in the sea – Diane didn't go in.

Took bus – ferry – ferry back to Darling Harbour to have our evening meal in the food hall of the shopping mall, which is a glass building reminding us of the old Crystal Palace. We ate Asian food. In this food hall, as in other food halls around the world, you buy your food from any of the surrounding food shops and take it to a communal dining area of tables and chairs. Then when you are ready for the sweet course you get up and select it from another food shop and sit somewhere else (if you wish) to eat. The whole place is ultra modern, but food is reasonably cheap.

We returned to our hotel by train, and then phoned our friend Don Riddle and arranged to meet him near his home at Narrabeen. Mike and Diane showed us 6 sets of colour prints of their travels round the world.

Night at The Kendall, Sydney.

Day 135. Tuesday April 27. Sydney.

This morning we went to the Australian Museum for 1¼ hours which wasn't really enough to see everything. It's a museum of natural history and the environment including Biology, Science, Aborigines and Geology. We then went back to the hotel for a quick lunch before meeting Michael and Diane for an afternoon visit to the Botanical Gardens. Then back to the hotel for an early take-away dinner as Pat and I had tickets for the Opera House. The performance was the Don Quixote Ballet which was very good – amazing dancing in the setting of the Sydney Opera House.

We are certainly making good use of our weekly travel pass to see Sydney and its environs.

Night at The Kendall, Sydney.

Day 136. Wednesday April 28. Sydney.

We left early this morning at 8.45 for Narrabeen by train and bus to see Don Riddle and his wife Shelley. He met us at 12 noon although we arrived 1¼ hours early which gave us time to walk round the town and beach area. The sands were beautiful and large rollers were coming in from the Pacific Ocean as there was quite a wind blowing. Don took us on a scenic tour, and we stopped at Bilgola Beach to swim in a sea water pool. Then on to Palm Beach just to look around. The weather had started hot and sunny, but deteriorated to cloud by the time we swam, and to rain by the time we returned to his home.

We had tea and when Shelley returned from work we all went by car to a restaurant in Manly which was very enjoyable. Afterwards Pat and I caught the 9.45 p.m. Sea-Cat back to Circular Quay, Sydney.

The area of our visit today north of Sydney was more hilly than the town and with the many bays and inlets made the views spectacular both for our afternoon drive and for the Sea-Cat journey back. We met Mike and Diane in their hostel for late coffee and looking at our photographs.

Night at The Kendall, Sydney.

Day 137. Thursday April 29. Sydney.

We went to the Power House Museum with Mike and Diane. It was Science, Technology, Space, Aeroplanes and lots of 'hands on' experiments – very enjoyable, but there were hordes of school children in many groups which lessened the enjoyment a little. Later we all went to Spit Junction to check out a meal at a Sizzlers restaurant for a farewell dinner and then on to Manly where we looked around beach and town and then returned to our hotels. Later we left again for Spit to have our farewell dinner.

Pat and I have had plenty to talk about during this week we have spent with Mike and Diane; they have been travelling for the last 6 months across America, the Pacific, and Australia, and will shortly be continuing on to Singapore and South East Asia before returning home around mid-August; Pat and I have spent the last month in Bali and Australia, and I have been travelling East from London since December, so we have many travel tales to swap!

A lot of today was spent waiting for and travelling on

buses and trains, but we have got to know Sydney! Returned to hotels about 10.40 p.m.

Night at The Kendall, Sydney.

Day 138. Friday April 30. Sydney.

We tried to walk to the end of Pott's Point with Michael (Diane had a headache), but we couldn't get to the end, called Garden Island, owing to Naval Dockyards and Ministry of Defence buildings. We ended up by walking through the Botanical Gardens again to Circular Quay to meet Diane at 12 o'clock. In the gardens we came upon an unfortunate gardener in an epileptic fit, so had to call another gardener for help. Met Diane and we all went for a ferry ride to Hunters Hill (Woolwich) and returned for Michael to keep his appoinment with the dentist at 2.30.

Meanwhile Pat and I went to The Rocks to visit the Observatory which was interesting with many 'hands on' experiments. After meeting up again at The Rocks tourist office we all then went to look at Pier One, which was a renovated pier with lots of restaurants and a large bookshop selling loads of books at reduced prices. Although Pier One was open it wasn't quite finished and there weren't many people, so it wasn't very interesting.

Pat and I had booked the airport bus for 6.30 p.m. so we said good-bye to Michael and Diane and left for the airport to catch the 21.15 flight to Tahiti.

Overnight Flight Sydney to Tahiti.

Day 139. Friday April 30. Tahiti.

We effectively put the clock back 24 hours after leaving Sydney and crossing the International Date Line, so we get two Fridays, both the 30th April. This compensates for all those single hours I lost each time I put the clock forward passing east through Europe, the Middle East and Asia.

It was an uneventful flight of 6½ hours and we arrived in the hotel at 8.45 a.m. We rested and swam in the hotel pool in morning. In the afternoon we caught a Truck (called Le Truck – really a truck converted to a bus) to Papeete as we

are 8 kilometres away, and had a look round the harbour
and rather scruffy shops and market. Well...this is not a
westernized country so we can't expect westernized
standards. We went into a bar for a drink and I got talking
to a local lady in French – she invited us both to play
snooker with her and a friend, but we declined. Weather is
hot at 26°c, and humid.

Pat and I had the hotel dinner buffet as we couldn't find
anywhere else to eat.

Night at Maeva Beach Hotel, Sofitel, Tahiti.

Day 140. Saturday May 1. Tahiti.

We were picked up by mini-bus at 9.15 a.m. for a whole
day tour. There were 9 people altogether. Visited Venus
Point, Botanical gardens, Gauguin Museum, Blow Hole,
Grottos and Waterfall. Also saw building works on South of
the Island for a new deep water harbour for cruise ships, to
be ready July 1994. We visited a Lagoonarium where we
took pictures of sharks and other fish, and then were
invited onto another jetty by some Tahitians who were
having 'a typical Tahitian party', as they called it! They had
their babies and young children with them, and invited 4 of
us to join them. They gave us free beer and musical
entertainment with guitars and shakers (dry rice in small
plastic Coca Cola bottles), and singing. Pat took a
photograph of two of their little girls, one of whom looked
like our granddaughter Roseanna.

During the tour we also visited a wine store where we
had wine tasting. It was really liqueurs made from local
fruits of all descriptions, and we had many samples and got
very merry and generally had a good time and lots of
laughing with our American fellow passengers. Pat thought
that we should have had the wine tasting at the beginning of
the tour to get us all merry at the start, because before this
no one had spoken much to each other.

Had dinner in the hotel after swimming in the pool and
sea for the last time. On the two evenings we have been in
Tahiti we have had dinner in the hotel open air restaurant
with roof only covering; here we had live entertainment of

traditional cultural dancing with fast knee knocking and bending by the men, and fast hip swinging by the girls. All dancers were in colourful Tahitian dress, girls in low hip skirts and many feathers in head gear, men with minimal clothing, all showing much bare flesh. The entertainment lasted all the evening and guests were persuaded to join in one session, but Pat and I didn't. So the evenings were very pleasant.

Night at Maeva Beach Hotel, Sofitel, Tahiti.

Day 141. Sunday May 2. Tahiti to Los Angeles.

6 a.m. Just phoned Qantas Airlines at the airport to re-confirm our flight to L.A. as everything was shut yesterday and I forgot to do it on Friday...but all was well, and we were picked up 6.45 for the airport. Had lunch and dinner on the flight of 7½ hours and arrived at the Airport Hilton Hotel late at 10.30 p.m. after waiting in inefficient and chaotic immigration lines, and taking over 2 hours to get out of the airport. The Hilton is a splendid hotel – on our 16th floor anyway – where, on arrival, we got complimentary coffee, biscuits, and fruit, and sat looking out at marvellous views over the airport and runways from the coffee lounge on our floor. There was nothing to indicate that it was free – but we weren't charged. We looked around other floors and couldn't see any similar coffee lounges!

Night at Airport Hilton Hotel, Los Angeles.

Day 142. Monday May 3. Los Angeles.

We came out of our room to go to breakfast at a fast food restaurant we had noticed near the hotel, when we saw the above mentioned coffee lounge open and there was a buffet breakfast laid out – cereals, Danish pastries, muffins, tea, coffee, fruit juices and fruit – we ate and drank, and weren't charged – although we did wonder how much extra this would add to our bill at check out time?

Pat and I re-arranged our luggage and did our packing – Pat was taking my case back with her plus a lot of my luggage, as I was going to be travelling as light as possible through North America – and arranged to check out at 2 p.m. which was considerate of the hotel as checkout is normally noon.

Around mid–morning we caught the hotel's shuttle bus to LAX (which is the town's abbreviation for the airport and written everywhere on buses, mini–buses, signs and cars) to check out Pat's Virgin Airline flight to London, also to get myself booked into a budget hotel for the night as the Hilton is too pricey! Eventually, after much talk with the hotel information desk clerk who was useless and knew less than I did about how to find and get booked into a hotel, I booked myself into a cheap hotel downtown. I even had to make, and pay for, the phone call myself.

We spent some time working out the airport transportation system for shuttle buses and vans (mini-buses), and returned to the hotel for a snack lunch by the swimming pool. Also we asked someone to take photos of us together as we were parting soon. We then had some more coffee and cookies in the coffee lounge (complimentary?), checked out, and for the last time took the shuttle bus to the airport. We weren't charged for the food and drink, and we never spent a cent in the whole 24 hours we were in L.A. We never understood why it was free because the accommodation was on a 'Room Only' basis. We will have to stay in the Hilton again some time!

I was about to embark on the final overland part of my round the world adventure and was decidedly apprehensive (with upset tummy) at saying good-bye to Pat and travelling alone for the next 11 weeks overland for ten thousand miles with no accommodation booked, only a route mapped out and a 30 Day Greyhound Canada Bus Pass. I seemed already to have been travelling a lifetime...! I guess this is no time for negative thinking...I must just get out there and do it...once I get started it will be alright!

We hung about for as long as Pat dared, and I decided I would use a mini-bus van for the journey to my hotel (these are actually private airport shuttle buses), as the taxi fare would be about $US25 and too expensive for my budget! I finally saw Pat through to the airport departure lounge at

4.30 p.m.

I felt a bit lonely walking back to the bus pick up point.

Monday May 3 continues in next stage.

Stage 6
Los Angeles to Anchorage

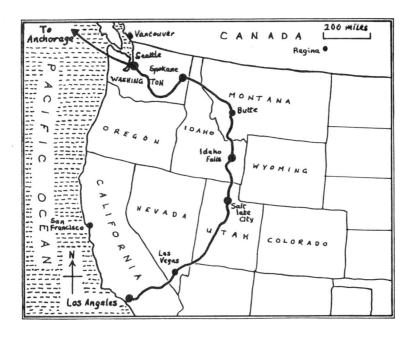

I spent 12 days travelling the western side of the United States, starting with the long train journey on the *Desert Wind* to Salt Lake City, where I stayed a few days doing family history research in the Genealogical Library of The Church of Jesus Christ of Latter Day Saints. This meant travelling west after this to get to Seattle and then Anchorage...going back on myself on my easterly trail round the world...but then I have allowed myself a few interesting diversionary activites to keep me sane...and thereby clocking up a good few miles more than the minimum 24,000 needed to travel the world at the equator! From Salt Lake City I travelled by Greyhound bus to Seattle, then a flight to Anchorage in Alaska. Distance 3,204 miles.

Day 142. Monday May 3 (Continued from Stage 5). Los Angeles.

4.30 p.m. After seeing Pat through the departure lounge for her flight to London, I phoned for a private mini-bus van. A mini-bus van only costs $US5 fare but it takes a long time as the system is that it circuits the numerous departure and arrival terminals 3 times so as to pick up as many 'fares' as possible. It took 2 hours to get to the hotel at 6.30.

I walked the 2 miles to the Union Railroad Depot and bought a ticket for the *Desert Wind* to Salt Lake City the following morning at 11.20, a 16 hour journey. I didn't particularly want to see any more of LA. Anyway, the hotel wasn't in a very salubrious area, so I decided to leave on the next train.

I caught a Shuttle bus/van back to the hotel. The only eating place open in the area was a no-frills old-fashioned restaurant with waiters in white shirts. I ordered Hot Pot with salad, and then 2 chunks of bread and a huge bowl of raw carrot and celery was served, which I noticed was on every table. The meal was a piled high plateful and I couldn't eat much of it!

The area round this hotel and restaurant is very quiet – skyscraper office blocks and many cleared areas of car parks which are almost empty, and no people about. I only saw two people on my return to the hotel, both asking for money and one appeared high on drugs...a bit scary! There are also a few expensive hotels around...it seems a peculiar area for hotels...maybe it's better in the daytime when there are more people about!

My hotel, The Stillwell, is staffed by Sikhs, but it's alright, clean, with T.V., bath and toilet at $US36. I notice it's in the YMCA list of hotels – although not a proper YMCA, it must be vetted by them to satisfy certain standards.

I spent a long time this evening doing my accounts, so that I can budget myself for the next 11 weeks. I have kept an account of my spending throughout each stage of my travels, and so far it's very close to my original estimate

made before I left home.
                    Night at The Stillwell Hotel, Los Angeles.

Day 143. Tuesday May 4. Los Angeles to Salt Lake City.

Union Railroad Station L.A. is a magnificent building built in 1939 – 'The Last Great Railroad Station to be built in America'. The architecture has Spanish and Art Deco styling with stucco facade, tile roof, and inlaid wood ceiling. It's often used for TV shows and movies. There was a TV crew there last night. It looks a bit Victorian as well, if that can be imagined! I took some photos, wheeling my luggage trolley around with me.

I caught the 11.20 Desert Wind. At 10 minutes before departure passengers are shepherded to the correct coach, depending upon destination. The train is quite super with double deck – I chose the upper deck. There is a special lounge/diner coach with buffet lounge on the lower, and observation lounge on the upper deck. You can understand why it's called Desert Wind because after the first hour we were in the desert. The roads I can see remind me of the ones I drove on in 1982 when I was here with Pat and our family.

4.30 p.m. Pat has been gone 24 hours and I guess has been home for about 12 hours. This train is the one that Michael Palin travelled in on his Round The World in 80 Days trip. We have been in the Majave Desert for some time now and have passed Barstow Station, and I saw 'CALICO' written on a hillside over the ghost town which we also visited in 1982. The lady I am sitting next to (around 35 years), and a man I spoke to in the queue for the train at Los Angeles (around 45 years), have both never been on a train in their lives – main line or city metro. I told the lady that it is fortunate for her that her 'first' is this Amtrak super train, and not the so called first class train in which I travelled from Amritsar to Delhi – she would have been put off trains for life!

Still desert and more desert..! Although there are quite a few plants, shrubs and lots of Yucca plants – because there has been a lot of rain in California this winter just gone, hence the desert is greener!

Las Vegas Station 6.45 p.m. I took a photograph of 'Circus Circus', a hotel which is really a huge leisure complex which we visited in 1982. The 'Strip' runs right alongside the railway. The train announcer said that we were stopping 15 minutes and if anyone gets off to go into the station casino...remember that casinos don't have clocks..! I walked along the platform, but no further. The train is due in Salt Lake City at 3.30 a.m. so I'll have a few hours wait in the station before looking for accommodation.

Overnight on Train and Station at Salt Lake City.

Day 144. Wednesday May 5. Salt Lake City.

The train was one hour late so I had less time to wait. Train arrived at 4.30 a.m. so had coffee and snack in Railroad Depot. I didn't want to walk into town before about 7.45 because it was dark and there were 'Street People' about. In the end I shared a taxi with a couple and left my luggage in the baggage room. This couple were on my train and had some hours to spare before catching a bus to another railroad depot. They were going to spend the time looking up their ancestors in the Genealogical Library, although they had never done any research before.

I checked in at the first motel on my list at 8.15 a.m. for $29. I was lucky to get in at such an early hour – a record I should think! Had breakfast at a nearby restaurant, like an up market Little Chef, then walked back to the depot, collected my luggage and took a cab to the motel.

The only reason I have come to Salt Lake City is to do family history research, so I am prepared to stay a few days and hope to get information on my ancestors that I haven't got already from my researches back in England.

I spent a few hours in the Family History Library getting to know what it contained and how to use it. A lot of computers were available, which seemed to have access to the names of all people christened and married world wide, where there is an original record of the event. I found details of some of my ancestors that I know of already, but not all of them...maybe there will be some records here that I have missed in England?

During the lunch break I went to a half hour organ recital in the Tabernacle which is just across the road from the library. The organ is the largest I've ever seen; it's recognized as 'one of the world's greatest instruments', and has 11,623 pipes. The Tabernacle is a masterpiece of acoustics as was demonstated by the organist before his performance, by dropping a pin, and then a nail, both of which I heard clearly at the back of the auditorium 170 feet away. The tabernacle was built in 1863, the base being oval and the roof dome shaped.

Salt Lake City is a spacious, clean and pleasing city, and is certainly worth visiting in its own right, apart from my genealogical research. The central Temple Square contains all the buildings of importance of the Church of Jesus Christ of Latter Day Saints (The Mormons). These are the Temple, Tabernacle, Visitor Centre and others, and all are kept spotless, and also set amongst beautiful gardens. The whole square is surrounded by a 15 foot wall with various gates which are always open to all in the daytime.

There are conducted tours throughout the day, one of which I went on. The Mormons are very welcoming and friendly people. They believe in the importance of family happiness, and that when they die they will join all their past family members – their ancestors, hence the importance they attach to collecting records of births, deaths and marriages, so they can find out who their ancestors were. The good thing is that they make all this information available freely to anyone who is interested.

It rains too much here, and it's too cold! I suppose it's bound to get colder the further north I travel!

Night at Covered Wagon Motel, Salt Lake City.

Day 145. Thursday May 6. Salt Lake City.

I spent a lot of time today investigating possible routes to Seattle, factors being Greyhound bus routes and where to stay. I want to book ahead so that I don't have the hassle of finding accommodation when arriving at a strange place with luggage. So I've found some motel chains that have properties on my route, like Flag Hotels where we stayed in Australia, then I know that standards will be of good quality. I've had a look round these motels in Salt Lake City, and decided on 'Motel 6'. I met a truck driver while I was looking round, and he said they were the best and the cheapest! I couldn't get a decent map of North West U.S.A. in the bus depot or the tourist office, so I had to visit the public library and take a photocopy of a page in an atlas.

This evening I went to a Choir rehearsal in the Tabernacle...free of course, as will be the 'on air' performance on Sunday morning. They sang some hymns that we sing at the Methodist church in Eastcote.

This part of the United States is in the middle of some stormy weather – rainfall is exceptionally heavy all over the west.

Night at Covered Wagon Motel, Salt Lake City.

Day 146. Friday May 7. Salt Lake City.

The city street verges and gardens in front of buildings are full of spring flowers, mainly tulips of many different colours. I've taken photographs. It really is a nice city!

Most of the day I've spent researching family history. I've enjoyed searching the computer files, but haven't turned up anything new. At mid-day I went to the observation floor of the highest building in town (26 floors) to look out and take photos, and of course it's an L.D.S. building – their office block. This is the local abbreviation for the Latter Day Saints, or Mormons, whose headquarters is here in Salt Lake City. As expected there was a friendly welcome and guide offered...free of charge! By merely mentioning the fact that it is free really highlights the fact that I am a little prejudiced in this respect, having not long ago travelled through the Middle East and Asia where friendliness was often suspect, with money really the motive. I suppose there is an ulterior motive here – to spread their belief, but it is very low key, as being happy and friendly seems to be their main theme in life.

Night at Covered Wagon Motel, Salt Lake City.

Day 147. Saturday May 8. Salt Lake City.

I have decided to stay for 4 nights to take full advantage of the research facilities offered at the genealogical library here. My probable route to Seattle is Idaho Falls (Idaho), Butte (Montana), Spokane (Washington), Seattle.

It's been wet most of the day with a thunderstorm, and then snow for about 3 hours and settling on pavements. I had to keep going out of the library to check bus times and routes, and phone ahead for tomorrow's motel stop. I'm finding the U.S. telephone system difficult to use. I have nothing much to report today...haven't turned up anything significant in my researches. I leave tomorrow on the 8.45 bus.

Night at Covered Wagon Motel, Salt Lake City.

Day 148. Sunday May 9. Salt Lake City to Idaho Falls.

10.30 a.m. Well, I'm on the move again on a Greyhound bus travelling north from Salt Lake City via Ogden, Logan, Pocatello to Idaho Falls. It's quite mountainous, as Salt Lake City has mountains all round except towards the Great Salt Lake. We have passed through one mountain range – lots of snow – weather reports say ski-ing conditions are excellent with deeper snow than most of the winter – unfortunately it's just about the end of the ski season and only privately organized ski-ing would be possible, as there would be no chair lifts etc. working.

Today the weather is fine with no cloud. The air is still cold but it is hot in the sun. I've bought a warm jumper in an end of season ski sale...I sent all my warm clothes home with Pat, thinking the weather was going to be warm from now on!

The Mormons. During my stay in Salt Lake City I naturally learnt some things about the Mormon Church. I went on a conducted tour of Temple Square, and yesterday visited the L.D.S. museum.

A lot of importance is attached to their temple in the

square, and the museum devotes a lot of space to its construction which took 40 years in the last century. It is a beautiful 4 spired building built of granite blocks. No visitors are allowed inside – only church members. All other religious temples in the Middle East and Asia have allowed visitors, so I couldn't understand why not here! When I have wandered round the grounds, the museum, and various buildings within Temple Square, there are many friendly guides always at hand to talk to. When I have asked questions and shown interest in their religion, the parting remark is always, "We will be very happy to arrange for a missionary to call on you." I say I'm too busy...time is limited...as I'm travelling! Many times I've been offered The Book of Mormon, but have declined graciously, explaining that I couldn't really afford the space in my luggage. This was really true...as I'm continually pruning my luggage, especially of books, which are heavy. All these guides and ushers that you meet are such friendly and charming people, especially the young women, of whom there are a large proportion.

Anyway, back to the Temple and associated topic! The Mormons believe that when you die you join your family (including all your ancestors) in heaven. Many of our ancestors, (probably 'most') were not baptized, and I presume it doesn't matter which religious belief they followed, but the Mormons strive to give all their ancestors the benefit of baptism for them to accept or reject as the case may be. Yes, they believe they have the ability of choice! If they accept it, they will be happy with their family, i.e. each ancestor's ancestors and descendants, and Jesus, for eternity. I don't know, as yet, what happens if an ancestor rejects baptism. Well, in order to baptize an ancestor, you must know who he/she was, i.e. their name, date of birth or Christening, which parish or district, marriage date, name and details of wife/husband, and your exact relationship to this ancestor. All this information has to be correct, and therefore checked and verified with other sources – just the same as when I'm collecting information about one of my ancestors, I want to be sure that I've found the correct one by verifying the details with at least one other source.

Now, this magnificent Mormon Temple here in Salt Lake City, which does not allow non-church members inside, has a large baptismal font of 'walk in' proportions and supported by many life size oxen (a historically significant animal). There is a life size model of this font in the L.D.S. museum, where I picked up much of this information. Baptism is so very important to the Mormons, and I understand that this font is used, not only for baptizing the living, but also for baptizing deceased ancestors by proxy, the proxy being the living descendants. Anyone recommending an ancestor for baptism must, of course, be a church member.

The importance of baptism and knowing who your ancestors were, explains why the L.D.S. have built up a gigantic world wide system for collecting details of births, deaths and marriages, and recording it on microfilm. The master copies of these films are kept in deep underground vaults outside of Salt Lake City, safe from natural and man made disasters. Copies of these films are made available to genealogical libraries worldwide, and these are what I have used mainly in my own family history researches in England. You can understand that with the increasing number of people becoming interested in their family history worldwide, the L.D.S. church has a great potential for new members. One of my 'friendly guides' did, in fact, tell me that a lot of new members come from this source.

The Mormons do not agree with drinking tea, coffee, or alcohol, so in the library and museum snack bars, only soft drinks are available. However, normal restaurants in the town sell tea, coffee, wine, etc.

I saw a wedding on the steps of the temple the other day, but I decided I had better not take a photo...I didn't want to offend...after all, I had to ask permission in India and such places where I didn't understand their culture and religion, before taking photos of people.

I am now in a town called Idaho Falls, and the area of the falls runs along the Snake River for about 400 yards. The banks of the river are all laid out gardens and picnic areas; there are many people strolling; children feeding ducks (including many Canada Geese); anglers. It's all very nice with everyone enjoying a sunny day...a Sunday afternoon.

I am staying in a very comfortable motel called 'Motel 6'. There are Motel 6's at my next two stops, Spokane and Seattle, so I shall make a point of staying at these properties, so avoiding the hassle of finding accommodation when arriving at a new town. Their advertising says they are the best and the cheapest, and having spent a lot of time searching accommodation brochures, it seems to be true!

Night at Motel 6, Idaho Falls.

Day 149. Monday May 10. Idaho Falls.

I have the whole day to spend here after checking out of the motel, as my bus departs at 11.20 p.m.

It's another glorious hot sunny day. I managed to get 8 dollars worth of 'quarters' to phone Pat from the public pay phone...I discovered how to do it yesterday. Then I walked down to the river and studied the falls to try to work out how power is obtained from the hydro-electric scheme, but a man told me that the actual tunnel the water drops through is further downstream. Also visited another L.D.S. Temple, only being allowed inside the public rooms, not the temple itself. It's right by the river and is a beautiful building. The documentary video I saw said that no non-members are allowed in from the moment the newly built temple is consecrated. I spent a couple of hours in the local public library which is of a very modern design set around a circular internal garden, and with a vast amount of space for each section.

I had a late dinner and went back to motel to collect luggage and get a taxi to the bus depot. Had to change buses at Butte at 3 a.m. The bus I boarded was dark inside and full of people sprawled over the seats...asleep, apparently, and reluctant to make room for anyone else. I eventually found a seat beside the only person sitting, although I didn't like the look of him in semi-darkness with his half shaven hair style. How wrong I was! He turned out to be an interesting travelling companion, and I had breakfast with him on arrival at Spokane. He was going on holiday to recuperate from a brain tumour operation, hence the hair style.

Arrived Spokane at 9.30 a.m. The same bus goes on to Seattle, which I will catch tomorrow.

Overnight on bus to Spokane.

Day 150. Tuesday May 11. Spokane.

The morning was taken up having breakfast, working out the local buses so as to avoid using taxis to and from motel which is 5 miles out of town, and sending some more things home to reduce my luggage weight. I have left my large bag in a lock-up until the morning, so I just have my rucksack to carry around.

After a few hours in the motel, I caught a bus back to town for dinner, as the only other restaurants near the motel are in expensive hotels. The whole day was hot and sunny. Spokane is a pleasant small town, with an impressive waterfall on the river just the other side of some sloping parkland. I managed to get a photo of this, and also of interesting sculptures of joggers on a sidewalk – life size and of bronze coloured metal.

If Spokane and Idaho Falls are anything to go by...I like 'Small Town America'.

Night at Motel 6. Spokane.

Day 151. Wednesday May 12. Spokane to Seattle.

I left the motel early intending to catch a bus to town, but at the bus stop a van driver stopped and offered me a lift. He was a man who I was chatting to yesterday at the same bus stop – he recognized me as he was driving past! Had breakfast in the bus depot cafeteria, and walked round the town a bit before catching my greyhound bus to Seattle.

1 p.m. Have just come through a place called Moses Lake, and am now crossing a bridge over the Columbia River which I saw a short while ago at the bottom of a

canyon. The river must be about 1 kilometre across. The countryside is low mountains and hills, all green covered scrubland and grass...desolate! This is not far from Canada, Spokane was less than 100 miles from the border. Since leaving Salt Lake City I have been in the Rocky Mountains, but now we have come onto the Columbia Plateau. The driver has just pointed out Mount St.Helens in the distance, which erupted in 1980, and Mount Rainier 14,410 feet.

I have decided not to go to Portland, although it's on my itinerary. It's difficult to find where places are situated in big cities when you're only in town one or two nights. In smaller towns the bus depot, railroad depot and motels are usually not far from each other. Another reason is that the route north from Salt Lake City, then west to Seattle, was supposed to be more scenic, and it has certainly been interesting country with snowy mountains, lakes, rivers and mountain passes.

We're in a heatwave here in the North West. Spokane yesterday was 89°F, the hottest since 1949 (presumably in May), and just now in Ellensburg at 2 p.m. it was 95°. I'm certainly getting extremes of temperature on my travels: London cold, Cairo hot, Turkey very cold at –20°C, India very hot, Nepal cool, Thailand and Malaysia very hot, Australia cooler, Tahiti very hot, Los Angeles cooler, Salt Lake City freezing and snow, and now very hot again here. I notice London is warm today at 73°F, and America is having extremes of temperature with 109°F in Arizona and 22°F in Wyoming.

Arrived in Seattle at 4 p.m. and left my luggage in a locker while I worked out how to get to the 'Motel 6', which is 20 miles from town, but near the airport, so I won't have far to go on Friday to catch my flight to Anchorage. It turns out that the bus I need stops at the motel and then goes on to the airport. I looked around town and had dinner in a pub with real ale, finally arriving at the motel at 8.30. It's on a busy road called Pacific Highway, semi-industrial, but with no eating places. On the journey I had good views of the Boeing Aircraft Company's works and hangars.

Night at Motel 6, Seattle.

Los Angeles to Anchorage

Day 152. Thursday May 13. Seattle.

I left early at 7.30 a.m. for the airport, to check out things for tomorrow i.e. bus stop and times, ckeck-in, and also to have breakfast. The airport is locally known as Sea-Tac because it lies between Seattle and Tacoma. I caught the bus to downtown Seattle where I intend to spend the rest of the day...there is nothing to do near the motel.

I arrived back at the motel at 8 p.m. and soon after, before it got dark, I walked down Pacific Highway (which looks like Western Avenue in the Perivale area of West London) to check again for eating places – thinking about breakfast. After about a mile I found a Taco Mexican Take-away, which wasn't suitable for breakfast, but I sat and had a cup of coffee. I had trouble ordering the coffee from the Mexican serving – I thought he didn't understand my English, but later another customer explained to me that the Mexican couldn't understand why I wanted coffee as I was obviously English and therefore could only want TEA!

I quite enjoyed my day in downtown Seattle, the weather was still clear and sunny although the forecast was 'rain later', but it held good all day. Seattle is surrounded by water: Elliott Bay is on the town harbour side which goes into Pujet Sound to the west; Washington Lake is to the east; then there are canals and a river.

Any city worth a mention has a high tower building, and here in Seattle it's called the Space Needle which is about 600 feet high, and has an observation floor, but I didn't go up as it cost too much. I will make a point of going up the one in Toronto. The Space Needle is a tower, rather than a building, like the Eiffel Tower in Paris, but more modern. It's set in a theme park area called Seattle Centre, with 'rides' etc. but the park was undergoing renovations so there wasn't much to do or see.

On the waterfront I went to see a Cinedome screening of The Eruption of Mount St. Helens, a volcano near Seattle which erupted in 1980. The Cinedome is a half dome shaped screen and the show was very realistic as viewed and heard from a helicopter at the scene. The initial explosion caused the biggest landslide in recorded history, blowing the top

1300 feet off the top of the mountain.

There is a mono-rail here which I went on from the Seattle Centre to a downtown area shopping plaza, where I had a coffee and then sat in the precinct square to eat my picnic lunch amidst all the water fountains, of which there are many around the city. These are really Designs in Water, or could be called Water Sculptures, and there were many such things in Sydney and other towns in Australia. I finished up with another dinner and a pint of real ale in the same Pub as yesterday.

Coffee in Seattle. Coffee drinking is a serious business in Seattle. You can't just ask for a black or white coffee; the bar person would look at you as if you were from another planet! First of all there are three sizes; they don't use the common words Small, Regular, Large, as used in fast food restaurants for drink sizes. This is coffee we're describing, so it's special! Coffee comes Short, Tall, or Grande. The different coffee drinks and their ingredients are:

Caffè Latte	–	Expresso, steamed milk, and foamed milk.
Expresso	–	Must be made fresh to order and drawn for exactly 20 seconds.
Caffè Mocha	–	Mocha syrup, Expresso, steamed milk, cocoa powder, and whipped cream.
Caffè Americano	–	Expresso with hot water added at the ideal temperature.
Expresso con Panna	–	Expresso and whipped cream.
Cappuccino	–	Expresso, steamed milk and foamed milk.
Expresso Machiato	–	Expresso (Latin American and Indonesian beans), and foamed milk.
Drip Coffee	–	10 grams ground coffee per 6 ozs water, brewed at precisely 195° F.

124

Milk can be Farm Fresh or 2% Fat.

Now, if you want a small drink, you don't just ask for a "Short," you have to make it sound better by asking for a "Single Short," and for a regular drink it's a "Double Tall," and for a large drink it's a "Triple Grande." These three sizes get 1, 2, or 3 shots of Expresso respectively. Thus, if you ask for "A Double Tall and Skinny Latte," this means when translated: Two shots of Expresso in a regular size cup with steamed and foamed 2% fat milk.

On coffee menus, for the health conscious, there is Decaffeinated coffee, and also Coffee of the Day. I haven't as yet ordered these, as all the others are much more interesting, and I'm only here two nights...so there isn't time to go through the coffee menu from top to bottom..! Maybe there will be coffee mania in Anchorage, so I can continue my studies!

The following quotation from a leaflet on a coffee bar counter sums up how serious is the matter of coffee drinking:

Good Expresso is nothing less than the pinnacle of coffee drinking. The beans should be ground and brewed immediately before serving, rewarding the drinker with a burst of flavor sensed throughout the mouth. This is not a cup to be lingered over, but rather provides one delicious mouthful to be savored momentarily, while the fleeting flavor is at its peak.

On the subject of healthy eating, the Americans appear to be very health conscious, because there are always many healthy diet dishes shown on food menus, but I think it must be only a token gesture (like the small print 'It can be damaging to your health' appearing on large advertisements for cigarettes), when I see the enormous unhealthy meals served up to most people in restaurants.

Night at Motel 6, Seattle.

Day 153. Friday May 14 Seattle to Anchorage.

I arrived at the airport early at 9.15 for my 12.15 flight, because I needed breakfast, and there was nowhere suitable to eat near the motel. I got up very early to walk the mile to the Mexican take-away to get a coffee, because the drinks machine at the motel wasn't working, but it was shut! This is the worst motel yet for inconvenience and things not working.

The flight to Anchorage was 3 hours and uneventful. Delta Airlines don't give free alcoholic drinks! Arrived at 2.15 p.m. Alaska time, which is 1 hour less than in Seattle. The distance was 1450 miles north west of Seattle, so I've gone a long way west on my eastward journey round the world from Salt Lake City, in fact I've gone west 38° of longitude, from 112° to 150° west at Anchorage. I've also come a long way north here at latitude 62°, and the sun sets only for a few hours. I went down to the coastal path to take photos of the sun setting over the Kenai Peninsula at 10.40 p.m. but it was still quite light at midnight.

I got booked into a motel by phoning from the airport, and they picked me up free of charge.

Night at Red Ram Motor Lodge, Anchorage.

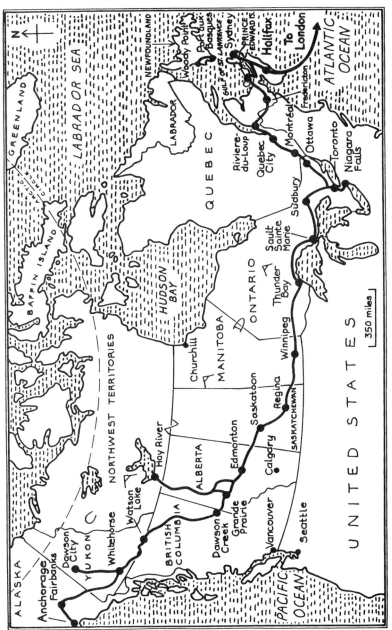

127

Stage 7
Anchorage to Halifax

I travelled alone on this continuous overland stage of the journey, starting in Alaska, and travelling across Canada to the Atlantic Province of Newfoundland, and finishing at Halifax, Nova Scotia, to catch a flight back to England. The first part in Alaska I travelled by train, and then it was bus all the way, using ferries to Prince Edward Island and Newfoundland. I visited all the twelve Canadian Provinces and Territories. Distance 8,492 miles, taking just over 9 weeks.

Days 154-156. Saturday-Monday May 15-17. Anchorage

I haven't done much writing these 3 days, just taking it easy, and not doing any sightseeing. On Saturday I went down to the railroad depot to check on trains to Fairbanks, and was just in time (8.30 a.m.) to see, and photograph, the last train of the winter schedule to Fairbanks, as it was pulling away..! The train I had wanted to be on! Back in England, when I had booked my flights for this trip, I had been unable to find out the 1993 schedules for this train, so had to guess, using last year's. It only runs weekly, and I wanted to catch a winter train as it would have been about half the fare of a summer train. The first train of the summer is on Wednesday, so I have bought a ticket for this.

However, Anchorage is a nice relaxing place to spend five days, and the weather is unusually fine for this time of year, although there are snow covered mountains on three sides. I've bought a senior bus pass and therefore pay only 25 cents a ride. I've been for a walk one afternoon on a coastal trail, but as in other places around the world, it was swarming with cyclists and roller blade skaters, but not many walkers. Nevertheless it was enjoyable, looking out over the sea, on a hot sunny Sunday afternoon.

This last stage of my trip – Anchorage to Halifax – I haven't planned in detail, I just have the general route in mind, and a Lonely Planet Guide, with no accommodation booked at all, so timing is very flexible...I just have to be in Halifax on the 18th July for my flight home. All the other information about the places en route, that I had at home – maps, brochures, timetables – I have not brought with me because they weigh too much! I rely on replacing them as I go. Ahead of me lies the longest overland journey I think I'll ever make, and when I look at the map of North America and see the thousands of miles I have to cover, the task I've set myself seems a bit daunting! Will I ever get to Halifax, Nova Scotia without getting tired and having to get on a plane for the last stretch? Will I feel like going all that way to Newfoundland to have a look around before I head for Halifax, which is what I plan to do? Well, I mustn't think these thoughts – just plan a few days ahead and enjoy each day as it comes!

I changed my accommodation after 2 nights to the Inlet Inn, a cheaper place at $US30, $10 cheaper, and I'm now in the middle of the downtown area instead of 10 blocks out of town. I have also arranged a stopover in Denali National Park on the way to Fairbanks. So it's Anchorage to Denali, stopover for a night in the park with a wildlife tour in the evening, then catch the train to Fairbanks the following day (trains are daily in the summer).

One night at Red Ram Motor Lodge, Anchorage.
Two nights at the Inlet Inn, Anchorage.

Day 157. Tuesday May 18. Anchorage.

There was an earthquake here in Anchorage last night...A couple of days ago I had been reading about a massive earthquake that hit Anchorage in 1964...when...just before I went to bed last night...a truck hit the front of the hotel! So I thought! I'm on the ground floor at the front, and the building certainly shook. The only explanation I could think of at the time was a truck out of control! I had no experience of such things! This morning's Anchorage Daily

News reports as follows:

> *Anchorage residents were shaken awake by an earthquake early this morning, but no damage or injuries were reported. The quake, which struck at 12.04 a.m. Alaska Daylight Time, was reported as two large jolts in quick succession. It was centred about 25 miles south of Anchorage and measured 5.2 on the Richter scale.*

The earthquake in 1964, which was 8.4 on the Richter scale, put a lot of the town in ruins, so this one was comparatively mild. There has also been earthquake activity in mainland USA, according to TV reports.

The day before, i.e. Sunday, the fire brigade was called to the hotel...the fire was in the kitchen where a frying pan had caught fire.

Today I took a bus trip to Eagle River (the town), and spent a couple of hours looking around. I couldn't get to Eagle River (the park), where there is a visitor centre, as there was no bus, and it's 12 miles from the town.

It's difficult to decide to go to bed when it's so light at 11.30. Although the sun was setting at 10.48 it doesn't go very far below the horizon.

Night at the Inlet Inn, Anchorage.

Day 158. Wednesday May 19. Anchorage to Denali.

12 noon. I am on the train to Denali, the weather is fine, and there is an observation car. This is a long train being pulled by two locomotives, and there aren't many passengers on it – the first train of the summer season. The scenery is interesting, but so far not so spectacular as the Canadian Rockies, but many degrees of wilderness and lots of snow.

I ordered a Roast Beef Roll in the dining car, and it came with soup, a plate of salad, and heaps of meat and cheese in a king sized roll.

The train was half an hour late at Denali, but my pick-up shuttle van driver was waiting for me...just me! I'm the only one staying at their camp, which doesn't open officially until next week. We were delayed at the station waiting for my luggage to arrive – it had been checked in just like on an airline, but we couldn't wait any longer as I had to get to my Wildlife Tour pick-up point at 5 o'clock, it was now 4.45. It never did appear because it was left on the train to Fairbanks. I'll check with someone in the morning to make sure they keep it at the Fairbanks depot for me to pick up tomorrow.

The wildlife tour was by coach, which was full of American travel agents. We saw moose and caribou. On the train earlier I saw a wolf swimming across a river, also more caribou.

My cabin is very comfortable – looks like a tent from the outside, but inside like a room, the tent covering for extra insulation. There are two double beds, electric light and heater. I'm the only one on the site – the manager and workers shut up the office and left at 10 p.m. I didn't sleep very well, I kept thinking I heard a wild animal banging on the door! Maybe a wolf or bear? These animals are around here, so I am told, and I've just read what I must do if encountering a bear while out hiking tomorrow on my own.

Night at Denali McKinley Cabins, Denali Park.

Day 159. Thursday May 20. Denali to Fairbanks.

I went on my hike this morning for 3 hours. I was apprehensive about the bears. The advice is: Talk while walking so as not to startle a bear. If one is about to attack, face it and stand still. When it stops, back off slowly until you are at a safe distance, then walk away. DO NOT RUN AWAY! If one actually attacks, curl up in a ball and play dead! If it still attacks, you must fight back! There ought to be Bear Confrontation Classes, but I haven't seen any advertised. I didn't see much wildlife, only ducks and birds. So unfortunately, I never saw a bear in the park, or even from the train yesterday.

I called in at the Railroad Depot to see what they had to say about my bag. It was there! They had sent it specially by road, although I didn't need it now. They were very apologetic and said I was famous now for having lost my luggage on the very first day of summer operation.

When I later arrived at the depot for departure to Fairbanks, about 30 of us passengers not on organised tours but travelling independently like myself, were kept waiting in a separate enclosure until a few minutes before the train was due. A young woman porter/announcer/guide (all rolled into one), whose job it was also to usher us to our correct coach, got out her clipboard and announced we were going to play a little game, and there would be prizes for the winner. Strange! By this time the train could be seen in the distance. Peculiar time to play games!

"I've got some questions for you," she said, "The first three you don't answer, but I want an answer for the 4th question, and the first correct answer gets a prize...here we go!"

"Which year was the Olympic Games held in Berlin?"

"Which continent is Japan in?"

"What is the capital city of Alaska?"

"How many miles is it from Chicago to San Francisco to the nearest 500 miles?"

Someone got the correct answer to the last question and received his prize, a bar of chocolate. This routine carried on until three similar prizes had been won, by which time the train had arrived and I realized that was the end of our Trivial Pursuits game...a pity! I was enjoying it. I suppose the first three questions were to divert your concentration from the final one. Maybe we could try this tactic when playing at home. Our Railroad Usher opened the gate and led us all to our respective coaches...and leaving me with a lot of admiration for the way the railroad staff in Alaska try to make their customers happy! Could we do this in Britain I wonder? I shall not forget the railroad staff at Denali.

I met a nice couple on the train to Fairbanks, who were in my group playing Trivial Pursuits. They were pianist and singer at an entertainment night spot in the park, and going to Fairbanks on two days leave – both from Nashville, Tennessee. We had dinner together.

I am staying in Bed and Breakfast accommodation called 'Peg and Jerry's'. Jerry picked me up from the railroad depot. They are Grandma and Grandpa to a little boy aged about 7 who asked me if we had television and telephones in England! There are so many people coming in and going out of the house, that I haven't sorted out who's who!

It's turned cold here in Fairbanks, near freezing point.
Night at Peg and Jerry's Bed and Breakfast, Fairbanks

Day 160. Friday May 21. Fairbanks.

It's still at freezing point again today with a nasty wind. I spent a lot of time today sorting out my next leg to Whitehorse. The 'Alaskon Express' bus service only started this week. Gray Line own this service and they promote an overnight stop at the Westmark Hotel in Beaver Creek, the halfway point in the 2 day journey, at $107 per night, but I've found a motel and booked my overnight stop for $54. I later realized these are Canadian dollars (it's just over the border) so it is less costly than the US equivalent. There isn't much choice in Beaver Creek with population of 100. The next bus to Beaver Creek is on Sunday, so I shall be on it. I spent some time in the public library looking at maps and books on the Alaska Highway which starts here in Fairbanks.

The town is very quiet as the season is only just beginning. In fact, the spring has just begun for Alaskans as the River Chena only became a river here 2–3 weeks ago. It's frozen over from October to May, and now the riverboat cruises have started for the tourists, this being one of the major attractions of the town.

I'm getting used to almost continual daylight now. (Similar to when Pat and I went to Spitzbergen last year). The trees and scrubs look nice all bursting out in the spring, the growth rate is fast here because of the 20 hours of sunlight each day. This increases until June 21st the summer solstice, when it starts getting less. Soon the grass and flowers will also start to grow fast.

Trivia information:

There is never 24 hours of sunlight here as it's 125 miles south of the Arctic Circle.
This is the farthest north I plan to go on my trip, at latitude 65° North.
Handicapped people are called 'Physically Challenged'.

During the 8 months per year freeze-up here they use the river as a road, driving vehicles and dog sledges on it for transportation. Airplanes land and take-off using skis. Just before and whilst thawing it becomes a bit dangerous, but because of the danger, local daredevils use it up to the last possible moment.
Night at Peg and Jerry's Bed and Breakfast, Fairbanks

Day 161. Saturday May 22. Fairbanks.

Yesterday I went by bus to visit the University of Alaska Museum, which is really the local history museum. The weather is much warmer today, 60° F, quite a contrast to yesterday.
This afternoon I went on a cruise down the river Chena for 3¾ hours. The boat was a large Sternwheeler paddle boat. Boats similar to this have been used on the river since the gold rush days of 1898. There were about 200 passengers, mostly tour groups from Holland America Cruise Lines and Gray Line of Alaska. All these people stay in the expensive hotels out of town, so I never see any in town, it's always deserted. We were taken ashore to an authentic native village, and saw bush pilots landing their aircraft on riverbank airstrips of about 30 yards long! I found this fascinating...and made a mental note that I must fly in a small plane! There are so few roads in Alaska that flying is a normal means of transport.
The River Chena empties into the Tanana River, which empties into the Nenana River 200 miles downstream. This in turn empties into the mighty Yukon River, and 1200 miles from here it empties into the Bering Sea.
Night at Peg and Jerrys Bed and Breakfast, Fairbanks.

Day 162. Sunday May 23. Fairbanks to Beaver Creek.

My host, Jerry, was going to give me a lift to my bus pick-up point at 8.15 this morning, but at 7.30, breakfast time, the house was still silent. I woke them up by going for a few minutes walk, banging the door behind me, and on returning ringing the bell for a long time, although the door hadn't locked itself anyway. All was well, I got breakfast and got my lift on time.

The Alaskon Bus Service to Beaver Creek carried two passengers – an Australian lady and me, although we picked up a staff member at Tok. So I've started my journey down the Alaska Highway. It's just another road really, but steeped in historical mystique.

When the Japanese bombed Pearl Harbour in 1941, it became necessary for the defence of Alaska to have an overland supply route from British Columbia, right through the Yukon to Fairbanks, Alaska. The construction of the Alaska Highway was one of the great engineering feats of its day. The task was formidable, but a one lane road was built in just over 8 months, from the Spring to the Summer of 1942 – 1500 miles traversing mountains, forests and rivers. Today it's mostly modern carriageway, but there are many places to stop which are of interest with historical mileposts and interpretive panels. We stopped where the Alaska Oil Pipeline crosses the road and I took a picture. This is another engineering achievement which has much space devoted to it in museums and tourist literature.

I am now at my motel in Beaver Creek which was virtually destroyed by fire in February, but I am in another building which survived. The new building is going up outside my window. Next door is a fire station...strange! You would think that living next to a fire station would make you safe from being gutted by fire...but not so! They never saw or heard the fire until it was too late.

Also in Beaver Creek is another motel, a hotel, a gas station, chapel, and the Royal Canadian Mounted Police, all spread along about 400 yards of road – that's all!

It's gone midnight and still light.

Night at Ida's Motel, Beaver Creek.

Day 163. Monday May 24. Beaver Creek to Whitehorse

I got up early this morning to explore and take photos of this place in the middle of nowhere. It's got a visitor centre (even the smallest of places have these), but it's not open until 9 a.m. by which time I'll be on my way. It even transmits local radio which I've been listening to on my short wave radio. There are more things here than I saw last night. There is a wildlife trail with realistic lifesize animal models set in their natural habitat with interpretive panels. As I haven't yet seen a live bear I took a photo of the model bear. There is a swimming pool which is shut this weekend including today Bank Holiday Monday (Victoria Day...surely the 24th May used to be Empire Day in Britain?).

Beaver Creek has impressed me..! While I was having dinner in the cafe attached to the motel, the proprietor's daughter came in with her 10 day old baby girl, and they were all cooing over this nice baby while I was eating, the only other customer! Seeing this happy family brought home to me the fact that these people of Beaver Creek are REAL PEOPLE and think nothing of living in this remote spot all year round. It's only just inside Canada near the border with Alaska. It lays claim to two things: it's the most westerly community in Canada, and it records consistently the lowest temperature in the North American continent, the coldest being –89°F (minus), which is –67°C (minus).

Ida's Motel and Cafe are open year round – they had just had a batch of T–Shirts made with the above two claims to fame printed on them for sale in the cafe, but the fire destroyed them all unfortunately.

The journey from Beaver Creek to Whitehorse today was across some of the best country I have seen, especially along by Kluane National Park with Kluane Lake on one side and mountains on the other. The lowlands are covered by short fir trees, stunted, but very green. These go on for miles and miles. Kluane Lake is large at about 50 miles long, and along the edge, varying from a few metres wide to a hundred metres, is the only water you can see, the thaw having just started after the long winter of ice. The various stages of unfreezing have produced varying colours of white, grey, and blue. So most of the lake is a sheet of ice and snow. There are lots of water birds about. In the distance are mountain ranges near and far, so, with clear blue skies the scenery is constantly changing. The only animal wild life we've seen on this two day journey is a ground squirrel!

The stops have been Delta Junction, Tok, Beaver Creek, Burwash Landing, Haines Junction, and now Whitehorse, capital of the Yukon Territory. This is a small town and spaciously laid out beside the Yukon River. The Visitor Reception Centre phoned for accommodation, although I told them who to phone as I had researched it from the Lonely Planet Guide and other tourist literature. It was about 6 blocks to walk, the farthest I've walked so far with my luggage – I'll have to be careful, as I don't want a recurrence of my back problem!

Polar regions, of which this area must be considered a part, have permanently frozen subsoil called permafrost. In this latitude that I've been travelling through in Alaska and the Yukon, there are 4 months of summer, so the topsoil thaws in summer and freezes in winter, but still manages to sustain plant and tree life. The ground below a couple of feet deep never thaws, and has been like it for thousands of years. The trees are stunted, they never grow very tall, not more than about 20 feet, and don't spread out sideways much as their roots cannot go down very far and the topsoil is frozen for 8 months of the year anyway. There are grasses and shrubs, and it's all very green now that spring is here and the trees and ferns etc. are bursting into life – rushing to make the most of the warmth and long days of the short summer. It's certainly a nice time of the year to be here, and with such long days, up to 20 hours daylight each day!

Inevitably, while building the Alaska Highway, some of the road was built on top of permafrost. The heat generated by the road traffic thaws the permafrost down to a lower level than normal, causing the road foundations to shift in the mushy thawed soil. So constant repairs are necessary. Repairs and improvements to the road can only be done during the four months of summer...they can't do much when it's eighty below! They only reckon to keep the roads open and clear during the winter, which is no small task! It's difficult to imagine how these people cope with such low temperatures and darkness throughout the winter months.

Night at 4th Avenue Residence, Whitehorse.

Day 164. Tuesday May 25. Whitehorse.

The 4th Avenue Residence is really a budget hotel, but it appears in the YHA handbook as 'Supplemental Accommodation'. The rates are very reasonable, also less 10% with my YHA card, although I would have got 10% as a 'Senior', but not both!

I have spent a lot of time today working out my schedule for the next few days. Long distance buses do not operate every day until later in June, so things need a bit of planning. I'm going to Dawson City for 2 nights by bus, then back to Whitehorse before I carry on down the Alaska Highway by the normal Greyhound Bus. So, no sightseeing today as I'm also too busy with other mundane matters like changing currency, checking on local bus times and stops for getting to the main bus terminal tomorrow, which is the other side of town. I'm only using taxis when I can't avoid it!

I do my route researching in the public libraries, sometimes also my writing. The public libraries in Alaska and also here in the Yukon, are very spacious and comfortable and somewhere quiet to go.

I called in to the Yukon Territory Tourism Head Office here in Whitehorse to look up John Pert, who I met at the London World Travel Fair in November 1991. He was in his office and was pleased I called in. When I told him I was going to Dawson City he immediately reserved me a room in one of the better hotels in the city, with compliments. So I won't have to stay at the budget accommodation of Mary's Rooms, which I hadn't yet reserved.

Night at 4th Avenue Residence, Whitehorse.

Day 165. Wednesday May 26. Whitehorse to Dawson City.

It's 335 miles to Dawson City on the Klondike Highway, which is one of only 11 main roads in the Yukon. It's the route that some of the gold prospectors took in the great Klondike Gold Rush of 1898, only they had to walk through this harsh country. The scenery from the bus was again wonderful, with many lakes, and forests of spruce and poplar, and all green. We stopped at Carmacks and Stewart Crossing for coffee and snacks.

Dawson City has been kept more or less in the same style as it was in its heyday during the gold rush days. All the buildings are wooden, pavements (sidewalks) are also built up in wood, and all the roads are gravel, but it's a living town, and the people are proud of their history. The Yukon River flows alongside the town.

Anyone who visits Dawson City must go to Diamond Tooth Gertie's Gambling Hall. Outside it looks like 1900, inside it's a bit more modern with One Arm Bandits and gaming tables. Staff are dressed as in 1900. $4.50 to get in and just buy your drinks and watch the entertainment.! Guess what? Diamond Tooth Gertie had me up on stage when I said I was from London, and sang sentimental songs to me while I tried to look as if I was enjoying myself. It ended with me having to take Gertie's garter off one of her dancing girls.

I sat with a guy from Edmonton who is in the gold business and is here for the Gold Show which starts tomorrow. One of the dancing girls happens to be his girl friend whom he met in Bali, she comes from Perth, W. Australia. So I had a good time chatting with these people. (I didn't know it at the time, but while I was up on stage he must have used my camera to take 2 photos of me. He didn't mention it, so the first I knew about it was two months later when I was looking at my developed photos back home.)

There is still a lot of mining going on here; I met a retired American who stays the whole summer, works on his own with his hi-tec mining equipment, and finds a little gold. But he does it for fun really. I also met a retired policeman who mines in his spare time. So the gold fever hasn't abated. I stayed for the second floor show as I had people to talk to, also had my usual flutter on the One Arm Bandits, put $5 in and got $6 out...not bad!

Night at the Midnight Sun Hotel, Dawson City.

Day 166. Thursday May 27. Dawson City.

A bunch of boys were whooping it up in the
Malamute saloon;
The kid that handles the music-box was hitting
a jag-time tune;
Back of the bar, in a solo game, sat Dangerous
Dan McGrew.

These are the opening lines of the poem 'The Shooting of Dan McGrew', by Robert Service, who was here during the Klondike Gold Rush. It's the same monologue poem that my father used to recite in the 'Roosters Concert Party' during the first world war in Alexandria. I have just learnt that it depicts the life in Dawson City during the gold rush days. Both Robert Service and Jack London the author are held in high esteem here, as they lived here in those days, and shared the rough and tumble of life, and of course, they both wrote about it. Jack London wrote 'Call of the Wild' and 'White Fang', which are both about those days. Both their log cabins are here as museums, and there are 'readings' of their works. Unfortunately, I wasn't able to get to any of these.

I spent some time this morning on a park seat in the sunshine, catching up on my journal, then it started to rain so I wasn't able to go to look at sights out of town, like a gold mining operation, and a climb to the Midnight Dome which is a hill overlooking the town where people congregate on 21st June, the summer solstice, to view the midnight sun over the town.

In the afternoon I managed to go on a guided walking tour of the town, although it rained quite heavily most of the time. The visitor centre here is a good base because they have free video shows, free coffee, and lots to look at while it's raining. The town is not very big, 10 minutes walk end to end. The people here, the locals, are proud of their town and its history, and it's been kept as much as possible like it was in '98. It brings in lots of tourists, and therefore revenue, and there are still 500 mining operations for gold, which is remarkable...but am I going to be able to see any? I haven't got a car and the rain is too heavy for walking miles!

Night at the Midnight Sun Hotel, Dawson City.

Day 167. Friday May 28. Dawson City to Whitehorse.

I went to Diamond Tooth Gertie's again yesterday evening, there being nothing else to do and it's a cheap evening out. I made sure I didn't get hauled up on stage again. I have been eating in a restaurant called Klondike Kate's, which despite its name, is a normal eating place.

It's still raining heavily, but I was determined to walk to the nearest mining operation 2 miles away. I was quite enjoying it, walking alongside the Yukon River in my wet weather gear, the river dark and sombre and the cloud base so low that I couldn't see the mountains...when a lady motorist stopped because she felt sorry for me and gave me a lift the rest of the way.

The young couple running the mine were just about to close it down because of the rain. Rain means no tourists and it's $1 to look over, $5 to pan for gold. Maybe they make as much money from tourists as from the gold itself! Anyway, I was shown round by the lady, and she explained the operations of dredging, washing, and panning. She refused to accept my $1 and kindly gave me a lift back to town.

I then, with some trepidation, started to climb up to the Midnight Dome. With trepidation, not because of the rain, but because the lady in the Visitor Reception Centre had warned me about THE BEARS again..."Had I read the bears leaflet?" I had! I was almost hoping to meet a bear because I hadn't seen one in all my time in Alaska and the Yukon. I followed the instructions in the leaflet – scraping my feet on the gravel, talking to myself, and generally making a noise so as not to startle a bear. They need plenty of warning of your coming. It was further than I thought – I only got half way up – It was still raining, so I turned back at a cemetery tucked away in the trees...is this where they buried the bear victims? I didn't see any wildlife, and it was getting late.

I came down and looked around the Jack London museum, and then back to the hotel for a snack before leaving for the airport to catch my flight back to Whitehorse.

The airport was hardly recognisable as such. It was a dirt track in a field next to the airport building. Rather than return to Whitehorse by bus, the same way I came, I decided to take a scheduled flight at $206 instead of $77 by bus. I've been thinking about a flight in a light aircraft since coming to these remote regions, and I would see all the marvellous scenery...and it would really feel like flying! I had to book and pay for the ticket 24 hours in advance, in order to get a special excursion fare, so I had to chance the weather. It was a 9 seater Beachcraft-80 with twin engines and two pilots. The flight was O.K. but we were soon in cloud and it was the same all the way until landing, so it was a bit disappointing, but different!

Night at 4th Avenue Residence, Whitehorse.

Day 168. Saturday May 29. Whitehorse to Dawson Creek.

I caught the Greyhound Bus at 12 noon for the 6 hour journey to Watson Lake, where I intended to stopover, but changed my mind half way through the afternoon and got the driver to re-validate my ticket to Dawson Creek where the bus arrives 9 a.m. tomorrow, this being the beginning, i.e. mile zero, of the Alaska Highway. Staying on the bus overnight is very useful as it saves on accommodation costs...you get a free night! This is my third such 'free night' since leaving Pat in Los Angeles!

If I'd stopped at Watson Lake I would have to have stayed 3 days as the next bus is not until next Tuesday. It would waste 2 days, thinking about my schedule in the weeks ahead. Also the magic has gone a bit regarding the Alaska Highway. The Greyhound Buses are unromantic and the driver doesn't point out interesting things as did the Alaskon Express drivers from Fairbanks to Whitehorse; the other passengers don't seem to care about the scenery and points of interest; I couldn't see out of the window much, it being dirty from the recent days of wet weather. So I decided to carry on until the end of the Alaska Highway, to Dawson Creek, doing 914 miles in one stretch.

Overnight on Greyhound Bus to Dawson Creek.

Day 169. Sunday May 30. Dawson Creek.

I managed to get into a Motel a few hundred yards from the Bus Depot, with 10% senior discount, total $37. It's hot and sunny here, shorts and T-shirt weather, even for me!

Dawson Creek is a bigger place than I had imagined, 11,000 population and such a long way from one block to another, very much spread out...there is so much space in this part of Canada!

The Visitor Centre in Dawson Creek has lots of history displays and videos depicting the Alaska Highway, also there's an art gallery with free coffee, and a museum to look around. There is a sprinkling of other visitors, all American, just starting their journey up the Alaska Highway, the normal way of doing it! I took a photo of a couple standing by the historic milepost zero, with their camera, and they reciprocated with my camera. I was able to tell them that I had taken a similar photo at milepost 1420, Delta Junction, near Fairbanks, the end (although my beginning) of the Highway, a few days ago.

Greyhound Lines run daily services east from here, so I'll stay two nights. In order to appreciate the Alaska Highway and this area generally, you need a vehicle so you can stop at interesting places. Most people visiting here seem to have an R.V. (Recreational Vehicle), another name for a self-contained camper/sleeper vehicle. There were some lovely spots near lakes that we passed yesterday in the bus, where it would have been nice to have stopped, but scheduled buses don't do that sort of thing!

My next objective, apart from my normal route across Canada, is to take a 'side' trip to Yellowknife, another gold rush town and capital of the North West Territories. It's the farthest north you can go in N.W.T. by road, and there is a scheduled bus service. I keep on wanting to go north! First Dawson City, and now Yellowknife, both not far from the Arctic Circle. Anyway, it will provide some extra interest, rather than just keep going east, and I would like to see the Great Slave Lake.

Night at Dawson Creek Lodge.

Day 170. Monday May 31. Dawson Creek.

I haven't done much worthy of note today, just taking it easy and wandering around the town and museums. There is an inexpensive restaurant attached to the motel so I don't have far to go for food. I have a T.V. and have watched a movie on each of the two nights. I have just learnt that this motel was a Travelodge until recently, owned by Forte, but for some reason it changed its status within the group and is now classed as 'A Property' of the Forte Group. It is of a good standard like a Travelodge would be, but not so expensive.

Night at Dawson Creek Lodge.

Day 171. Tuesday June 1. Dawson Creek to Grande Prairie.

I left Dawson Creek by Greyhound Bus at 10 a.m. for Grande Prairie, the first stage of the journey to Yellowknife, a two hour ride. At the Grande Prairie Bus Depot I discovered that my schedule to get to Yellowknife was no good because my copies of the Greyhound timetables were incorrect, so I had to work out another, also fitting in a 2 day farm visit to people I met on safari in Nepal who live near Grand Prairie.

I left my main luggage in a locker at the bus depot and walked downtown heading for the tourist office to research my trip and make phone calls to motels. When I went to make the phone calls I found I had left my invaluable Lonely Planet Guide in my bag in the locker, so I had to go back to the bus depot. But it was shut, and opened at 11 p.m. for the 11.45 bus which I was catching. It was now 3 p.m. so I had a lot of time to waste.

The weather was very hot and dry. I ate in Eaton's department store restaurant and spent some time in a bar where everyone was watching an important ice hockey match on television. Montreal were playing, and I had to wait a long time to get served as even the bar girl couldn't tear herself away from the excitement. While here I telephoned many times to Claudette, who lives nearby, and separately to her brother on the farm, both of whom I met on safari in Nepal three months ago. At about 8.30 I finally got an answer from Claudette. Fortunately she wasn't doing anything for the rest of the evening, and came to pick me up. She took me to a restaurant for coffee and cookies and a chat. She works in the local hospital as a physiotherapist, and said she would ring her brother Gilles to let him know I would be back in this area again at the weekend. I had been invited to stay on his grain farm.

Claudette gave me a lift to the bus depot by 11 o'clock, and I retrieved my Lonely Planet Guide and phoned Yellowknife for accommodation. One motel was full, another was $140 per night, and others in the list were similarly expensive. So I gave up the idea of Yellowknife – my new schedule would have got me there at 10.55 p.m. tomorrow, which is too late to start looking for accommodation. I settled for Hay River which is on the south side of the Great Slave Lake arriving at a convenient time in mid-afternoon. This is the interchange for Yellowknife anyway.

Overnight in Service Station and Bus to Peace River.

Day 172. Wednesday June 2. Hay River.

It needed three buses and two changes to get here. The first bus at 11.45 p.m. from Grande Prairie dropped me at 1.15 a.m. at a 24 hour gas service station with cafe. Three hours later at 4.15 a.m. I caught the next bus to Peace River, arriving at 6.30 a.m. and then a bus departing at

7.45 for Hay River. So that was a hectic night's journey! I easily got booked into a motel by phone and took a taxi, there being no such thing as local buses in this remote region.

Hay River is a small town with population of about 3000 and very spread out. The roads are gravel and very dusty in the heat. There is a 16 storey skyscraper, the tallest building in North West Territories, and it looks incongruous amongst all the other small town buildings. There is also a bright purple secondary school, which is rather odd. The population of North West Territories is only 54,000, but it covers a vast area: over 3¼ million sq. km. – about a third of Canada. It's all wilderness country, and geographically either arctic or sub-arctic.

Night at the Migrator Motel, Hay River.

Day 173. Thursday June 3. Hay River.

Hay River lies about 4 kilometres up river from the Great Slave Lake, and today I walked to the lake 5 kilometres each way this morning, and 4 kilometres each way this afternoon because I found a better approach through a forest road. The lake is about 450 x 200 kilometres, so really like a sea! The ice started breaking up only a couple of weeks ago, making about 200 yards of clear water at the edge. It's quite a sight! Approaching from a distance from slightly higher ground, it looks like an ice cliff out to sea, because there is little perspective when looking at the shimmering ice. As you get closer it becomes clear that it's just flat ice to the horizon. There are lots of birds on the many sand bars near the shore.

The shore is a graveyard for dead trees. The beach is covered in tree trunks! It's only the trunks that have survived the journey in the sea, I suppose. Between the trees is all the broken up bark and some branches, with sand patches here and there. It's difficult to walk as it entails climbing over the trees. The lake must have lots of fallen trees in it, caused by storms, and then at a later storm they get washed up on some far shore. I took some photos of this phenomenon. There are two distinct lines of trees, each parallel with the shore line, supposedly from two different storms, like tides of the oceans which deposit garbage on the beach at different levels, only this garbage is huge trees up to 60 foot long – I measured the longest one I could see. I don't think there are tides here, so they will only get eroded over years.

The beach I visited on this morning's walk was a picnic area where people go swimming in the summer, but this was littered with small trees as well. I spoke to a lady in the Greyhound Bus Depot who told me that her son went swimming in the lake yesterday...it's apparently the macho thing to do immediately after 'break-up'.

'Break-up' is the term used for the melting and breaking of the ice on lakes and rivers each spring. It's an important event because it heralds the coming of summer warmth and the end of the winter freeze-up. In Fairbanks and Dawson City there are prizes of thousands of dollars for the nearest guess of the time of 'break-up' on the river, similar to a lottery. A participant chooses a second of a day. The exact second of break-up in the hour of a day is determined by hanging a mechanical device in the water from a bridge just before the water freezes in the Autumn. The device is connected to a clock on the shore. When the device is set free in the water by the breaking up of the ice in the spring, it stops the clock on the shore, and that time is 'break-up' to the second!

The mosquitoes here are big, with a bite to match. I know that I've said this before in this journal, but they get bigger as I travel from Alaska to the Yukon and now North West Territories. This morning I forgot to take my repellent with me, and was attacked on the back of the neck...in the mid-morning sun as well! There is a joke that goes around these parts – an old joke, because it was told in the days of the building of the Alaska Highway which had to be built in the summer, between spring and autumn, before winter set in. It goes something like this:

Two mosquitoes have rendered a victim semi-conscious on the floor of a tent...

First mosquito to second mosquito: "Shall we carry him
    outside?"
Second mosquito: "No, the big ones might get him!"

They call them 'man-eaters'. I met a man on the train from
Anchorage to Fairbanks who was going into the Alaskan
wilderness to do gold panning for a week. He'd never done
anything like it before. The thing that worried him most
was not the bears, nor the snakes, nor the sub-zero night
temperatures...but the man-eating mosquitoes that he'd read
about! He had grown a thick beard to help protect his
face.

Night at the Migrator Motel, Hay River.

Day 174. Friday June 4. Hay River to Peace River.

This trip seems to be keeping me fit – I'm out in the
open a lot, either walking around town or along river
banks, and always searching for somewhere to eat. If I do
too much, like yesterday's 18 kilometres, my back gives a
little protest – but it's O.K. this evening. But my feet are
wearing out! I got blisters on my heel when I did a long
walk along the coast at Anchorage a few weeks ago, and it
never really healed. Yesterday it got bad again, although I
always put a dressing on it before long walks.
I think I go to bed too late, with the darkness not
coming until about midnight, and I always write this journal
at night, but it takes longer than I think! I plan to walk
tomorrow as this seems an interesting place for walks –
Peace River (a town), in Peace River Valley. I left Hay River
at 8.30 this morning, and arrived here at 4 o'clock this
afternoon, and this motel is only 200 yards from the bus
depot – I checked it out during a 45 minute stop-over en
route for Hay River two days ago. In spite of it being only
200 yards away, I left my heaviest bag in a lock-up in the
bus depot as I'm only staying one night, and I'll pick it up
tomorrow on departure. This is all very mundane stuff and
not specially interesting, I'm sure!
There are a few places that I've been to in the USA and
Canada that were not on my itinerary...it made travelling a

bit more exciting, suddenly deciding that I must go somewhere, then working out how and when to go. These places are: Idaho Falls and Spokane in the U.S.A. and Dawson City, Hay River, and Peace River in Canada. I've always got my eyes and ears open for further possible 'side' trips!

There are some places on my itinerary where I never stayed: Portland USA, Watson Lake and Fort Nelson in Canada. Portland I missed because I changed my route completely to get to Seattle. I didn't stay over at Watson Lake although the bus stopped for half an hour, enough time to visit the tourist centre, post a letter, and take a photo of the 'Forest of signs' where, during the building of the Alaska Highway, a homesick soldier stuck a sign up of his hometown. The idea caught on and now there are hundreds and hundreds of such signs. I came through Fort Nelson but didn't stay over.

Night at the Crescent Motel, Peace River.

Day 175. Saturday June 5. Peace River to Falher.

I walked up a hill overlooking the town where there is an historical memorial to a person called 'Twelve Foot Davis', a local pioneer who staked a gold claim 12 feet wide between two existing claims and made a fortune. The view over the Peace River town, river and valley is quite exceptional, with the river snaking away into the distance, and there are many islands. The town looks like a miniature town from this height, with 'matchbox' cars and a train going over a bridge, reminding me of Bekonscot Model Village in Buckinghamshire.

In the afternoon I caught a Greyhound bus to Falher, about 40 kilometres south of here, and was met by Gilles whom I first met with his sister on Safari in Nepal 3 months ago. He runs a grain farm here. His parents, Rene and Louise, also live here, but in a different house, which is where I am staying. His sister Claudette, who I met a few days ago in Grande Prairie, is also here with her boy friend as it is the week-end. There is also a young Frenchman who is learning farming to help with his credentials when he starts up a farm in France. We all sat down to a home cooked meal and then I was taken on a tour of the farm in a pick-up truck.

The farm is not one continuous piece of land; it's made up of 'quarters', each of which is ¼ of a square mile, for example, if this is an area of land :-

X				X					X
X	X			X		X		X	X
	X	X						X	
					X	X		X	
X					X	X			

The quarters with an 'x' would be their land and in fact the distance between their furthest apart quarters is 12 miles, which takes about one hour in a tractor.

Night at the Roys' Farm, Father, Alberta.

Day 176. Sunday June 6. On the Roys' Farm, Father.

This farm is about 460 kilometres N.W. of Edmonton.
Today is a day of recreation and no work. I thought that farmers worked 7 days a week, but it's not so with grain farmers, there are no cows to milk, no cattle to look after, so when the weather is fine they go out for a picnic.

We all went on a water-ski picnic, to Lake Winagami, about 45 minutes drive away, packed up with food for lunch and dinner, pick-up truck towing the water-ski boat on a trailer, and Rene and Louise's R.V. in which I travelled. We arrived about 11.30 and took over a picnic site of picnic bench, table and barbecue oven. We had hot dogs for lunch and home made beefburgers for dinner. The weather was hot. All the people who were at dinner at the house yesterday were there, and they seemed to know everyone else who was there.

It is a very close knit small community, they are all inter-related and French speaking, their ancestors came from Quebec 125 years ago and these people are their descendants. They all speak French together with explanations sometimes to me in English, but when speaking they will often switch to English and back again to French, sometimes in mid-sentence. They are bi-lingual because as small children their parents always spoke in French, and then they picked up English when they went to school. Three villages round here are mainly French communities.

I went out on the lake a few times in the water-ski boat, but only as assistant – I decided that I'd better not do water-skiing because of my back, although the temptation was hard to resist with people saying, "Come on – have a go!" from time to time. The lake was really so muddy, otherwise I would have gone swimming. I went walking and bird watching. Anyway, I had a good day, and we arrived back at 9.30 p.m.

Night at the Roys' Farm, Father, Alberta.

Day 177. Monday June 7. Father to Edmonton.

This morning I was taken by Gilles' father Rene on a tour of their Alfalfa processing plant, and was shown everything from the cutting of the plant to the finished product in pellet form, which is used as animal feed. The pellets are mainly exported to Japan where they do not have enough land for grazing cattle, so they buy this high protein animal feed from Canada. Alfalfa is a plant with clover-like leaves and flowers, and grows about a foot high. Rene runs the Alfalfa plant, and Gilles runs the farm growing wheat and other grain.

In the afternoon I went on a chemical spray run with Gilles and drove the pick-up truck to help a little. I also went on rides in a huge tractor, although I didn't drive it. Gilles took me to the village to catch the 5.20 bus to Edmonton. As I was arriving in Edmonton late, about 11 p.m. I have already booked a room in the Y.M.C.A. by telephone.

Night at the Y.M.C.A. Edmonton.

Day 178. Tuesday June 8. Edmonton.

I had a bad night! I was woken twice in the night with a raging itch on my legs. I thought I was being bitten by some insect in the bed – the more I itched, the more I was convinced it was something in the bed. So in the morning I complained to the receptionist about it, and insisted he gave me another room.

I realized later, having talked to a pharmacist about it, that it was delayed action bites from insects that were bothering everyone at the lake on Sunday. There were certainly swarms of them in the evening, in spite of the wood fire burning, but on leaving the lakeside, I promptly forgot all about them until this morning, when it suddenly dawned upon me...so I went immediately to a pharmacist. But 32 hours delayed action!! I had to apologise to the receptionist as I had more or less told him there were bugs in the bed! Both my legs are now literally covered with bites and it's giving me a bad time, but I've now got this anti-histamine cream which eases it slightly.

Nevertheless, I took a bus ride out of town to West Edmonton Mall which is a place you must visit if in town, because it's the largest shopping and recreational complex in the world according to the Guinness Book of Records. It contains all the large department stores, many food halls, cinemas, water park with simulated waves onto a large beach, water chutes, ice rink, submersible adventures, dolphinarium, a Fantasyland Park similar to Alton Towers in England, with roller coasters and suchlike, and a hotel. All this is under cover and air conditioned so that you can come in the heat of the summer or in the cold of the very harsh winter, and still be comfortable. I found the whole place fascinating and could have spent more time there.

It's hot in Edmonton, and I'm in shirt sleeves all the time. There are a few elderly men in this Y.M.C.A. - residents fallen on hard times. One man, who got his name in the newspaper, has been a resident here 30 years, another man 14 months.

Downtown Edmonton is not very large, all business buildings, banks, government offices, and department stores, but easily walkable. The suburbs stretch for miles, making it a large town.

Night at the Y.M.C.A. Edmonton.

Day 179. Wednesday June 9. Edmonton.

In the morning I did mundane things like washing and drying as there are laundry facilities, but no washing powder, which is normally sold at the reception in small packets, but they'd run out, so I washed by hand and tumble dried.

As I was not keen to go sight seeing round yet another town, I went to the convention centre where there is a dinosaur exhibition called 'The Greatest Show Unearthed' – it was quite good, with lots of audio visual displays and real samples from dinosaur digs. They really have dinosaur fever here as there is a lot of publicity about a new movie called Jurassic Park. There are large dinosaur footprints painted on sidewalks, which if followed will lead to the dinosaur exhibition – there is a Dinosaur National Park in Alberta where dinosaurs have been found, so the people here have good reason to be interested in the subject.

One part of the exhibition, a large part, is especially for children. I didn't stop at this, but it looked good with many 'hands on' digs and Dino competitions. The whole show was well organized with local volunteers on duty at each exhibit to explain and entertain. It's a mobile show launched in Edmonton but later moving on to Toronto, then Japan.

I went swimming here at the Y.M.C.A. pool, which gave me temporary cooling relief for the raging itch still on my legs.

Night at the Y.M.C.A. Edmonton.

Day 180. Thursday June 10. Edmonton to Saskatoon.

I met Roy at the Edmonton Bus Depot and we travelled together on the 8 a.m. bus to Saskatoon.. Roy is an Australian from Melbourne who arrived in Anchorage the day after I did, and is travelling eastwards across Alaska and Canada on more or less the same route and timing as me. I only knew this when I just happened to meet him in Edmonton yesterday. I had already met him on the bus from Whitehorse to Dawson Creek – he also has the same Canada Bus Pass as me which he bought in Australia.

At Saskatoon we checked in at the Patricia Hotel which appears in the Youth Hostels Handbook as 'Supplemental Accommodation', and is a good budget hotel. We shared the cost of a twin room. He is off early tomorrow morning to Regina, but I'm staying over a bit longer. Saskatoon is a nice town with the South Saskatchewan River running through. I shall have a further look around tomorrow before moving on.

In the evening I walked around the town with Roy and we had dinner together. It was nice to have a friend for a change, after travelling alone for the last five weeks.

Night at the Patricia Hotel, Saskatoon.

Day 181. Friday June 11. Saskatoon to Regina.

I checked out the possibility of getting to Prince Albert National Park by bus, it's a few hundred kilometres north of Saskatoon. I still haven't seen any bears! But I decided not to as it's not covered by my Canada Bus Pass.

I walked round Saskatoon and alongside the river, and visited a museum 'Meewasin Valley Centre', about the history of Saskatoon. This is a pleasant small town with river and valley – like Peace River Valley of last week – both of these places I would like to visit again some day with Pat.

I caught the 1.30 p.m. bus to Regina and to this hostel, the first proper hostel I've been to, so it was a new experience for me. Although I had joined the Youth Hostels Association back in England I was always a bit apprehensive about actually doing it, being content so far to stay in motels...until I met Roy who always stays in hostels when possible, and he's about the same age as me. I noticed he had already booked in earlier, and in fact there were only the two of us in the dormitory, with a total of six in the hostel.

It's a beautiful building of historical significance, the

inside being also in immaculate condition, and no shoes are allowed to be worn inside. I decided to do the thing properly and cook my own meal – it took me 2¾ hours to shop and cook, all on my own in the kitchen and dining room. They have Safeways here! but it took me ¾ hour to find it! It's lights out and quiet by 11 o'clock, which is early for me, so I had to be quick.

Night at Turgeon International Hostel, Regina.

Day 182. Saturday June 12. Regina.

This hostel closes between 10 a.m. and 5 p.m. so I had to leave by 10 o'clock. I walked round town to find the Post Office, but it closes the whole weekend, so I went up a tall building 'Saskpower', (Saskatchewan Electricity Co.) where there was an art exhibition and observation gallery. It was raining so I didn't take any photos – no one else was there, only a security guard in the lobby. There is a folk song festival in the park in the centre of downtown, so I listened to this while having my picnic lunch.

My fellow traveller Roy checked out this morning, and is heading for the Winnipeg hostel, where we shall probably meet tomorrow. He doesn't stay long at places, preferring to travel fast.

In the afternoon I went by bus to the Royal Canadian Mounted Police museum, and had my photo taken with a lady corporal who had just 'passed out' from college and was resplendent in her ceremonial dress. I also took a photo of a RCMP wedding. I walked around a local beauty spot Wascana Centre, which is a large urban park with many ducks and Canada Geese – I took a close up photo of some baby geese which should be good if it comes out! Visited the Natural History Museum which had a large display of dinosaurs...this town also has a dinosaur fever like Edmonton had, because many fossils were found in these parts. There was a very life-like Tyrannosaurus Rex, titled 'Megamunch', which moved and roared, set in an environment of 65 million years ago. I think all five grandchildren would have been a little frightened of it, being so lifelike! All these places I have visited today were free!

I then set about the task of shopping and cooking for dinner, sharing the kitchen with an Englishman and his Swiss girl friend. There are only five people staying here tonight. Later, in the evening, when I had retired to the lounge to write this journal, a girl student told me about the delights of staying at the Ottawa Hostel which used to be a jail, with original cells as rooms, including the death cell which is haunted. The hostel has organized tours for tourists and, she said, I must stay there as it's an experience not to be missed, especially if you get allocated the death cell!

Night at Turgeon International Hostel, Regina.

Day 183. Sunday June 13. Regina to Winnipeg.

I caught the 8.05 a.m. bus to Winnipeg, the journey uneventful, arriving 5.30 p.m. There are always stops every 1½ to 2 hours throughout the day, although there is a rest room on all buses.

The important topic in the news throughout Canada these past few weeks is the resignation of Prime Minister Mulrooney, and the Conservative Party Conference, which is in Ottawa today, to elect a new leader of the party, and therefore a new prime minister of Canada for at least the next 4 months when there will then be a general election.

We have just heard that Kim Campbell has won the election and is therefore the first lady Prime Minister of Canada. Everyone has been bunched round the television here at the hostel in Winnipeg waiting for news of the vote, and all Canada is very excited about it...it's now 7.30 p.m.

I arrived at the hostel at 6 p.m. just in time for a barbecue dinner in the garden...unexpected but welcome, as I didn't have to bother about shopping and cooking! Free too! My friend Roy was already there as expected.

Accommodation here costs $12 with free coffee. I don't think I'll bother about Motels or Hotels anymore as there is a hostel in most of the places I want to go from now on. Everyone is very friendly and it's very clean and hygienic. Quiet time is midnight here so I've been able to finish this journal.

Anchorage to Halifax

Night at Ivy House International Hostel, Winnipeg.

Day 184. Monday June 14. Winnipeg.

Manitoba, Saskatchewan and Alberta, in fact all the way from Edmonton, have been flat country, agricultural land, and in Saskatchewan the fields are mainly wheat. The fields are now green with the early crops and there has been rain during the last few days which was much needed all over Canada. On the Roys' farm at Falher where I stayed, they were desperate for rain, so I hope they have had it there too! The fields were very patchy with lots of weeds overtaking the crops in growth.

Today it is cold in Winnipeg, not normal for this time of year, with a cold wind. Apparently it's often windy in Manitoba and in the Winter this puts the temperature down to minus 60°F quite often.

In the downtown area a large area of stores, shopping complexes (above and below ground), Post Office, Library, Banks, Insurance Companies, are all connected by second level and/or underground walkways which are climate contolled, so you don't have to go out in the cold streets at all. I used these today for my downtown visit as I hadn't come prepared for the cold, it having been so warm yesterday, remembering the barbecue we had on the outside patio at the hostel.

In the afternoon I visited the Forks, an historical heritage site which is a nice place to go when it's warm, with gardens and lawns laid out by the river, and open air theatre and buskers performing. This is where the Assiniboine River meets the Red River, but there was no one walking outside, and nothing happening, as it was too cold. Historically this is where people have met for fur trading and other trading activities for 6,000 years, and is where Winnipeg itself was founded. There is a turn of the century stables building which has been renovated and turned into an exciting modern covered market place, with shops and restaurants.

I also visited St. Boniface Basilica and museum alongside, which is the oldest surviving building in Winnipeg, built of oak logs. I saw the tomb of Louis Riev, who was executed by the state in the 1880's for treason. He was the founder of Winnipeg Province, and a national hero because he basically stuck up for the rights of the native peoples when the early pioneer settlers started to come and claim the territories where the natives had lived and hunted for generations before.

As I had become a dinosaur fan in Edmonton, where there was big publicity for a dinosaur exhibition, I went to see the movie Jurassic Park, which had its preview in Edmonton only last week. It's Steven Spielberg's latest movie with very realistic dinosaurs created by computer graphics, and all-round sound. I enjoyed it, but had a headache when I came out. Dinosaurs were noisy creatures, it seems, especially when they were chasing humans. Incidentally, the movie is billed with the dinosaurs as the stars, the humans as supporting cast!

Night at Ivy House International Hostel, Winnipeg.

Day 185. Tuesday June 15. Winnipeg to Sault Ste. Marie.

I checked out of the hostel at 8.15 a.m. and caught the 10 o'clock bus to Sault Ste. Marie, my next stopover. This will be my longest bus journey so far at 1,380 kilometres, arriving 6.30 a.m. tomorrow. Canada is certainly a big country! Weather is sunny and warm today. After about 2 hours travelling east from Winnipeg, the terrain has changed to forestry and lakes and hills, which is more interesting than the prairie lands to the west. We stopped for lunch at the Greyhound Depot and restaurant at Kenora, a resort town and very pretty, on the lakeside of the 'Lake of the Woods'.

Later! We are now in Ontario and it's all hills, views, lakes, and rock outcrops...there are over a million lakes, rivers, and streams in Ontario. We stopped in Thunder Bay for refreshments and I went for a walk to get fruit in a supermarket. I did originally think of staying over here for a night, but glad I didn't as it's too industrial.

A deer ran across the road in front of the coach, and we saw two young moose when it was nearly dark. It's 9 hours driving and 700 kilometres from Thunder Bay to Sault Ste. Marie, along the northern and eastern side of Lake Superior. This was from 9.30 p.m. to 6.30 a.m. so I saw late evening and early morning scenery.

Night on Bus along Northern Shore of Lake Superior.

Day 186. Wednesday June 16. Sault Ste. Marie.

Sault Ste. Marie sits strategically on the narrow stretch of water joining Lake Superior with Lake Huron, called St. Mary's River. The USA is on one side, Canada on the other. There are 4 working locks on the USA side raising or lowering ships the necessary 7 metres of height difference between the lakes. The locks were built so that shipping could navigate right up to Thunder Bay to pick up the grain harvests from middle and western Canada. There is also a lock on the Canadian side which is not used commercially, but is now an historical site which I visited for photos and views of the rapids, which are quite extensive in the middle of the river.

I spent a lot of time on the waterfront promenade, which is interesting with views of the USA a half mile away connected by a road and rail bridge.

Night at the Algonquin Hotel, Sault Ste. Marie.

Day 187. Thursday June 17. Sault Ste. Marie to Sudbury.

The Algonquin is listed in the YHA Handbook as Supplemental Accommodation. It's really a hotel giving cheap rates for YHA members. Comfortable and clean.

Visited the Sault Ste. Marie museum which is small but has well-put-together displays. The town is important historically, due to its position between Lake Superior and Lake Huron.

It's raining today and the water looks forbidding out on the St. Mary's River. I caught the 12 noon bus to Sudbury, arriving 4.30 p.m. and it took me 2 hours to fix up accommodation.

The greyhound bus depot is out of town, but the driver

stopped downtown for anyone who wanted to get off there, and I decided I would. That was fine, but it was raining and I had all my luggage with me...

Firstly I must find where I am on my inadequate map in a tourist brochure...find a shopping mall to get out of the rain...find a rest room...a telephone...the International Hostel is out of town to the north...the Greyhound bus depot was east...I phoned the hostel...no answer – only an answerphone, "Leave your number, we'll ring you back". Oh yes! shall I wait here in this phone booth one hour or two? No, don't bother, I'll ring another hostel in town that used to be the official Canadian hostel...I don't know why it's changed...no answer..! try later...or shall I walk the four blocks and just turn up..? no, they might not be there anymore...try a motel...must find the restroom...this was very difficult. By this time I wished I had gone on to the proper Greyhound Bus Depot as they always have luggage lockers and this chasing about could have been done without carrying all my luggage. Find another phone box...ring a hotel from 'Lonely Planet Guide'..."Sorry we don't have rooms anymore, only apartments"...try another hotel..."Sorry, full up"...try another...no answer...I'm fed up! Then I saw a coupon in a tourist brochure for the Belmont Inn which is just out of town to the south. $44 plus tax = $50. They had a room and the receptionist told me which bus I needed. I was fortunately already outside the bus transit depot.

As far as getting booked up for the night is concerned, today in Sudbury was the most difficult so far. As luck would have it, as a form of compensation, this motel is the best one I've stayed in so far! The staff are very friendly and helpful and they have a good and cheap coffee shop for dinner and breakfast. The young lady receptionist, who is very friendly, introduced me to another guest, a young man from Finland, who is in Sudbury for 6 months learning to fly helicopters, so we had an interesting chat. I told the receptionist about my ancestors coming from Sudbury in England, but she had never heard of that town..

Night at Belmont Inn, Sudbury.

Day 188. Friday June 18. Sudbury.

I caught a local bus to downtown to look around and do some shopping and Post Office jobs. In the afternoon I walked to Ramsey Lake on the edge of town where there is a science museum called Science North with lots and lots of 'hands on' exhibits. There wasn't time for me to appreciate everything, so I'm going back in the morning with the same ticket. Sudbury is noted for its nickel mining, but I'm not sure if I'll have time to go on the mine tour.
Trivia:
Everything in this part of Canada has to be in two languages, English and French. For example, on entering Bell Park there is a sign:

PARK   BELL   PARC

All food and drink descriptions have to be in two languages. For example, a can of ginger ale has printed on the label in English:

CANADA DRY
GINGER ALE
THE CHAMPAGNE OF GINGER ALES

Also in French:

CANADA DRY
GINGEMBRE
LE CHAMPAGNE DES GINGER ALES

Also everything else on the label, e.g. ingredients and nutritional information, is in the two languages. All printed matter, like for example, postal rates information, and anything else that is official, must be in the two languages. The Canadians must use twice as much paper as other countries!

Night at The Belmont Inn, Sudbury.

Day 189. Saturday June 19. Sudbury to Toronto.

Walked to Ramsey Lake and spent 4 hours in Science North which is a marvellous place. The traditional idea of a museum has 'gone out of the window', at least as far as science is concerned, and the 'hands on' approach to exhibits as in the Science Museum London, has been carried a stage further. There are laboratories for the visitor, and fossil hunting and cleaning. But what fascinated me was the geology...

In geological terms the area around Sudbury is called a basin, and geologists are fairly certain that the cause of the Sudbury Basin was a huge meteorite that struck 1,800 million years ago. This resulted in a large upheaval of the rock strata, bringing an almost limitless amount of nickel to within mining distance of the surface. Sudbury is also on an earthquake fault line (like the San Andreas fault line in the San Francisco area), and earthquakes have played their part in this upheaval of strata. There hasn't been an earthquake here for millions of years, but the interesting thing is that Science North is built on this fault line called the 'Creighton Fault'. The entrance is through a tunnel hewn out of the solid rock, and at one end of the tunnel, you can see the fault line...it's actually two distinct edges in the rock about 40 feet apart. The rock between these edges is the rock that moves in an earthquake. Although there hasn't been an earthquake for millions of years, a device, in the form of two rods of iron, has nevertheless been embedded in the rock in such a way as to detect any rock movement in the future. They can never be too sure!

In the geology section a geologist answered all my questions and they had a seismograph working which had recorded the earthquake I had felt in Anchorage on May 18th, although they had not kept the detailed 'print outs'. All sections of the museum have a specialist in attendance, also a lot of volunteer workers at hand to answer general questions. The whole concept is orientated towards explaining things 'people to people', as well as the normal descriptive materials and text. There are many video shows and computers to help.

I happened to be there when there was a special celebration with speeches to open a new section on the museum's 9th birthday, with free cake and beverages. There are a lot of children's things – the driver of my bus to

Sudbury said he often leaves his two young children there for an afternoon. They have special 'sit-ins' for children when there is an eclipse of the sun or moon, and make a fun event of it – all night if necessary. While I was there an announcement came over the loudspeaker asking people to go outside to the open space area by the lake to watch the launching of a 6 foot rocket over the lake. The Canadians certainly make science fun!

I left the museum at 2 p.m. in order to get back to the motel to pick up my luggage, get two local transit buses, and catch my Greyhound Line bus at 5 p.m. to Toronto.
Night at the International Hostel, Toronto.

Day 190. Sunday June 20. Toronto.

It's raining and there is low cloud here in Toronto – can't even see the tops of normal buildings, let alone the Toronto CN Tower.

I met someone in town, a Glen Campbell, whom I had met on the bus from Sudbury yesterday and he bought me a coffee and English Muffin. He used to be a flying instructor, then a driving instructor, now he delivers cars.

I couldn't think of what to do in Toronto – I was just wandering around dodging the rain – the Eaton Centre shopping mall was closed, and so were most shops – no point in going to the waterfront (Lake Ontario) as there was low cloud, mist and rain, visibility poor – no use going to the top of the CN Tower for the same reason. I was still wondering what to do...Then I noticed there were crowds of people walking in the same direction as me on this wide sidewalk, young people, old people, families with children – no one was going the other way! Where were they all going? There must be some event! Now there were people pouring out of the subway – touts selling tickets! The Sky Dome! I could just see it in the distance, a large covered stadium. There was something on at the Sky Dome! It was a baseball game. I just went with the crowd – there was nothing else worth doing. So I bought a $5 ticket and saw The Toronto Blue Jays v The Boston Red Sox.

The Sky Dome itself was worthwhile seeing anyway,

because I had noticed from The Lonely Planet Guide there were conducted tours. The preliminaries and razzmatazz during the game were entertaining, but I had had enough after two hours, although there was still another hour to go.

Night at the International Hostel, Toronto.

Day 191. Monday June 21. Toronto.

I spent the morning in Toronto locating the KLM offices and getting my flight ticket actually replaced with a new one for the revised date of my flight home from Halifax, now the 18th July, also locating the Don Mills Post Office where mail may have been sent to me. I discovered that it was miles out of town – a bus and train ride away, so I just phoned them – there was no mail! I was misled into giving my family the Don Mills P.O. for mailing me in Toronto. I was given to believe it was a convenient downtown Post Office. I will phone them again when I return to Toronto from Niagara.

I had lunch in the revolving restaurant at the top of the CN Tower. It costs $11 to go the observation deck, or buy lunch and get the elevator ride free. I bought lunch for $19, so I got lunch and a beer, and VIP treatment for the extra $8. The weather, fortunately, was clear for most of the hour, whereas the previous day the top was in mist all day.

I spent two hours up there, also looking at the exhibition of construction photographs, and taking the elevator up a further 30 levels to the highest observation deck. The views were terrific! Toronto is on Lake Ontario, so it's just like a coastal town, with some islands off the coast.

I caught the 4 p.m. bus to Niagara Falls, arriving at the International Hostel at 6.30. Later, in the evening, I walked with a group of hostellers to the falls, to see it lit up after dark. Unfortunately there was a slight drizzle, and this combined with the mist coming off the falls, made visibility rather poor – but there is always tomorrow..!

Night at Niagara Falls International Hostel.

Day 192. Tuesday June 22. Niagara Falls.

Today was hot and sunny and a marvellous day for looking at the various parts of Niagara Falls. It really is an incredible sight, and there are so many aspects and views to see. I was mainly on the American side where I spent 5½ hours. I had to get a new visa which was a bit of a problem as I should have kept the one I got on arrival at Los Angeles from Tahiti, but the Canadian Immigration people tore it out when I entered Canada 4 weeks ago at Beaver Creek.

I took heaps of photos so I should get some good ones. Towards the end of the afternoon I was brave enough to go to a walkway directly in front the Bridal Veil Falls on the American side, in a long plastic raincoat and special shoes, with an organized group. The force of the water was so great that I got soaked right through and could hardly see to walk. We were not, of course, under the full force of the middle of the falls, but it seemed like it, just being on the edge, and there was certainly a weight of water hitting us. We had to pay for this madness! I'm glad I didn't go prepared to take photos, I wrapped my camera in a plastic bag. It would have been like trying to take photos in the worst rain storm imaginable! Fortunately it was hot when we all came back out into the sun, and I dried off in about one hour.

There were a few other 'wet making' daring things to do, but I had had enough! Apart from the falls, there were hundreds of metres of rapids to be seen from islands and bridges, and then the awesome drop of 180 feet, and you can get so frighteningly close to the top edge, just a few feet! Then there is the noise of the thunder of millions of gallons of water dropping to the lower river...and the huge pall of mist...and the rainbows creating a half circle...You must all come to Niagara Falls one day.

I took a bus ride along the Niagara Gorge to Niagara-on-the-Lake and back, using the local transit bus service called People Mover.

Night at Niagara Falls International Hostel.

Day 193. Wednesday June 23. Niagara to Ottawa.

I seem to have become a confirmed hosteller, it's certainly very convenient, I don't have to search for somewhere to stay, it's cheap, and there are people to talk to, even some older people, not many, and none quite so old as me, but I've got used to it, and the hostel system, so I'm happy.

To-day I'm in prison! The County Jail! Actually the Ex-County Jail, right in downtown Ottawa. It was the prison until 1972, and the last person executed was in 1869, and his legend and ghost still live on. The building is a heritage sight so is not allowed to be changed inside or out. My bedroom is a cell for 4 prisoners (hostellers), complete with iron bar doors, and iron bars on the windows in the corridor. It's really remarkable how it still looks like prison.

The condemned cells and death cell are not actually used as dormitories except that the death cell is made into a bedroom of sorts if any hosteller chooses to accept 'The Dare', and stay locked in the death cell 12 hours from 9 p.m. to 9 a.m. with no personal effects except the clothes he or she stands in. You get a chance to come out at 2 a.m. when the security guard comes round. There are no lights, and about 60 people have done it since 1973 when the hostel opened. These people have written their experiences in a log book called The Patrick Whelan Log, this being the name of the person last executed in the prison by public hanging. Those hostellers who stay in the cell 12 hours get the night's accommodation free.

The place is said to be haunted, and many of these brave people have heard things in the night. Some of the staff have had extra-ordinary experiences on the top floor where the condemned and death cells are located. There are historical tours conducted round the building, one of which I went on today.

Night at Ottawa International Hostel.

Day 194. Thursday June 24. Ottawa.

Ottawa is a beautiful city, I suppose it was made to be so because parliament is here. I spent the morning going round the parliament buildings on a conducted tour, and then in the grounds and gardens which are beside the River Ottawa. The afternoon I spent mostly in the National Gallery which is an ultra modern glass, steel and concrete building. Inside is interesting when you suddenly come into garden courtyards and water courts.

I wandered unknowingly into a special modern art exhibition, and although the exhibits were not revolting or disgusting, they were outrageous to me in that they were allowed to be called art! This so called art was exhibited in enormously grand galleries, and each room had only one or two exhibits: a wall of a room had been re-plastered to put a bump in it, entitled 'A pregnant woman', a hole cut out of another wall, I forget the title. A large single colour screen with a yellow edge entitled 'Untitled'. The inevitable bricks, 37 of them just positioned on the floor in a straight line in a huge gallery, the wall plaque said that they were purchased from someone in 1979, just like an art gallery might buy a work of art from some notable institution, but you could buy these from the local brickyard! Who were they trying to fool into appreciating this so called art? I asked an attendant if she could help me into viewing these bricks in an artistic way. She was unhelpful! I moved on to the next room. A thirty foot length of rope about 3 inches thick, of the type that would be used for tying a large ship to a dockside, was positioned 'tastefully' on the floor of this huge gallery!

There were sculptures by Anish Kapoor, an Indian who studied in London, which were similarly outrageous to me. Also normal paintings by impressionists and others going back many centuries as in any art gallery.

Night at Ottawa International Hostel.

Day 195. Friday June 25. Ottawa to Montreal.

In the morning I crossed over to the other side of the

River Ottawa to Hull which is in the Province of Quebec. There is a Museum of Civilization here which seemed interesting but I didn't have time to go in. I walked back another way via a second bridge and was just in time to see the changing of the guard outside the Parliament House. The guards' ceremonial uniform is the same as in England. There was also a troop of kilted guards.

This is the first ceremonial change of the summer and it happens each day throughout the summer, so I was lucky to see it. The 'new' guard then took to the streets complete with band and I followed with many other people, as they seemed to be going on the road back to my hostel. There was a great sense of occasion with the marching and the music, everyone taking photos and traffic brought to a standstill.

I left the marchers near the hostel, went straight back to check out and caught a local bus to the terminus to catch the 12 noon bus to Montreal.

10.30 p.m. Montreal is just like France, everyone speaks French in the streets although in shops the assistants will speak English if necessary. The weather is hot and humid as it was in Ottawa, and most people are wearing shorts. This is a big city, second biggest to Toronto, and very modern. This hostel is in a residential neighbourhood which is very French – there are many pedestrian precincts full of cafes spilling on to the sidewalks.

Night at the International Hostel, Montreal.

Day 196. Saturday June 26. Montreal.

The weather is very hot and humid, similar to Bangkok and Indonesia, although Montreal is a long way from the tropics! There is no air conditioning in hostels, and with 16 people in a not so big dormitory, it is very uncomfortable at night.

I have been round the old town and waterfront this morning – fell asleep on the grass by the waterfront – I'm continually having cool drinks to combat the heat. I caught a ferry to Île Sainte-Hélène, a small island in the St. Lawrence River, which was the main anchor site for

Expo '67, although now it is parkland. In the park, built for Expo '67, is the Biosphere, the largest geodesic dome in the world, representing ¾ of a sphere with a diameter of 250 feet. The trip to the island was very pleasant as there was a cool breeze blowing on the river and also on the island. I caught the Metro back to Montreal.

Montreal itself is really one big island, situated between the St. Lawrence River and the River of the Prairies, so there is plenty of water around which makes a city interesting.

I had dinner out and bought fruit for breakfast. I haven't been cooking dinner at the hostels since the first one at Regina. It's too difficult buying for one person, and doesn't in fact work out much cheaper, eating out being cheap anyway. I eat bananas and oranges for breakfast and lunch, sometimes soup for lunch as well.

I'm leaving Montreal tomorrow and I haven't seen much at all...the first evening (yesterday) I had a problem finding a store to get a new battery for my camera, although I had a spare, it was the wrong sort, and today I haven't done much because of the heat, and now it's nearly time to leave.

I've just discovered the fact that there is an underground city here for the very purpose of getting out of the heat in the summer, and out of the cold in the winter, but somehow I missed knowing about it. There is a 29 kilometre underground network of pedestrian precincts and walkways serving all the major stores and connected to food halls, theatres, railway and bus depots, metro stations and hotels. Yesterday I could have escaped from the unfriendly weather and spent the day in this city within a city! Another time maybe! I must go to bed as it's 11 o'clock (Quiet Time).

Night at the International Hostel, Montreal.

Day 197. Sunday June 27. Montreal to Quebec City.

Before I left Montreal I climbed to the top of Mount Royal Park, which lies at the back of the town not far from the hostel. There is a lookout at the top where I admired the view over the city and took photos. Arrived back at the hostel in time for the latest check-out at 9.30 a.m. At this time the dormitories are locked until late afternoon, meaning all luggage would be locked in! This is the earliest lock-up time in the hostels I have so far stayed at.

I boarded the local bus and then the Metro to the Terminus Voyageur bus depot, where I caught an Orleans Express bus to Quebec City. The Metro trains in Montreal are unique in that they run silently on rubber wheels!

4.30 p.m. Arrived at the Quebec hostel which is in the centre of the old city. There is no pretence here at being Canadian, everything looks French and everyone speaks French – it is more French than Montreal. There is so much of interest here in the old city that I haven't been out to the modern part yet.

Night at Centre International de Sejour de Quebec.

Day 198. Monday June 28. Quebec City.

This morning, after Post Office jobs and a little shopping, I took myself on a self-guided walking tour of the old city. It's certainly a very interesting city with a history from 1608 when Samuel de Champlain first settled here and began the process which eventually made Quebec City the provincial capital and beacon of the French language and culture in North America. The city's fortifications, begun by the French and completed by the English in 1871, have been preserved until this day, making Quebec unique in being the only fortified city in North America.

The wall still surrounds the city, and the Citadel, completed 1850, is still in operation and occupied by the Royal 22nd Guards Regiment. You'd think and feel you were in England, looking at the guardsmen on duty, but that's where the feeling ends, because in town there is no pandering to anything English as mentioned before in this journal. Street names are in French, all notices in shops, shop names, restaurant menus are all in French. You only hear French spoken, and are greeted in French, although staff in restaurants usually will speak English. I thought all Canada had to display things in the two languages, but it isn't done in Quebec Province, including Montreal.

Here in Quebec City I really forget I'm in Canada, dragging out my French phrases, but I'm enjoying it.

There is a big debate in Canada about the future of Quebec Province, one side of the argument saying it should be independent of Canada, the other saying it will never work. Many Quebecois can't speak English, the schools only teaching it just like any other subject, and not an important one! Consequently, if parents want their children to become proficient in English they have to pay for private lessons. To get on in business or politics in Canada or internationally one must have good English, and for an independent Quebec to work, more emphasis must be placed on English in the schools, so that more of future generations can be groomed in international affairs and politics. The debate on Quebec is really about language and culture – should their national identity be French or Canadian? A further problem is that an independent Quebec would split Canada down the middle, it being right in the geographic centre.

I dodged out of the rain into the Château de Frontenac, which is a hotel built in the style of a French chateau. It is enormous and dominates the old city. There was a conducted tour just starting, so having nothing better to do in the rain, I joined the tour. Two historic conferences were held here in 1943 and 1944, attended by Winston Churchill and Franklin Roosevelt at the invitation of Canadian Prime Minister MacKenzie King. There are photographs of this meeting in the lobby.

In the evening, back in the hostel lounge while I was writing this journal, I heard a familiar Australian voice...it was Roy, my Australian travelling friend whom I last saw in Winnipeg just over two weeks ago. He's been travelling fast again, having already been over to P.E.I. (Prince Edward Island) and back. He told me of his travels and updated me on things I must see on my way to P.E.I. He is on his way to America, and then to England where he said he would look me up on my return.

Night at Centre International de Sejour de Quebec.

Day 199. Tuesday June 29. Quebec to Rivière-du-Loup.

I am on the bus to Rivière-du-Loup with the ever widening St.Lawrence River on the left. The countryside is green and wooded with rolling low hills and grassland, and fields of crops.

This morning before setting off for the bus depot I went with Roy to see the changing of the guard at the Citadel. It was very cold and I had come out unprepared for the weather again, so I came away at half-time (my phrase), after the old guard was dismissed and before the new guard came on. Each half lasts 25 minutes of drill and inspection, drill and inspection. I went back to the hostel to get warmed up before leaving for the bus depot.

I caught the 1 p.m. bus to Rivière-du-Loup arriving 3.30 and after a long exhausting uphill walk arrived at hostel at 5 p.m. I was told immediately by the receptionist lady that someone was organizing a bird watching trip by car up the coast to Cacouna, on the St. Lawrence...Did I want to go? Of course I wanted to go..! I'd specially chosen to travel along the coast of the St.Lawrence because I like rivers and birds. There were four of us altogether – a young Swedish couple, a young woman called Jennifer who was organizing the trip, and myself. Jennifer works for the Government Environmental Program and is staying at the hostel.

We saw many types of birds including Night Herons, but also saw Beluga Whales (White Whales) which are about 4 metres long, also spent some time studying a Porcupine family. We managed to see the above interesting wildlife in spite of the haze caused by millions of mosquitoes. They got me round the ankles under my socks where I hadn't sprayed! Back at the hostel someone said it was because I ate too many bananas. I wonder! I have certainly eaten bananas frequently on my travels through Alaska and Canada, and I never seem to get immune from their bite.

I had thought the St. Lawrence River here was about 4 kilometres across to the other side, but I was way out! Jennifer, (the environmental program girl) says it's 25 kilometres (16 miles), and it is, because I checked it on the map, nearly as wide as the English Channel! It's deceptive because the coast on the other side is mountains and fjords, and therefore clear to see at that distance. Some river! It gets wider of course further downstream where the other side is not visible.

Night at Auberge Internationale de Rivière-du-Loup.

Day 200. Wednesday June 30. Rivière-du-Loup.

I haven't seen much of this town, only a quick visit to the City Hall Tourist Office, the rest of the day I spent on or by the river. In the morning I walked alongside the river admiring the views and saw more Beluga whales close inshore. Had lunch in the port café, and caught the 2.45 ferry to the other side at Saint-Siméon, and then back without disembarking – called a 3 hour cruise, for $10.90.

There were more Beluga whales near an island in the middle. The only other ship I saw was a fishing trawler. The ferry held about 400 people and 100 cars. It was a very pleasant afternoon cruise. The walk back to the hostel took about one hour. I had soup and a snack as it was too difficult to cook a proper meal.

In the evening there was an organized excursion to Aster Scientific Station and Observatory which is 60 kilometres away at Saint-Louis du Ha! Ha! We were taken by mini-bus by Guylou the hostel manager. On the guided tour we were shown wind energy, solar energy, meteorology, geology and seismology. They had a record of 'my earthquake' in Anchorage on May 18. The weather was perfect for night sky observation, so when it was dark we took turns to look through the observatory telescope at the Moon, the Milky way, Jupiter and moons, and a Nebula. We could see the craters on the moon, and Jupiter looked as big as our moon is to the naked eye. It was marvellous! Aster is essentially a working scientific station and not a museum, although there are some museum exhibits.

Arrived back at midnight...we had drinks...I phoned for a taxi for 3.30 a.m...bed at 12.30...up at 3 a.m. All this very tight, not much sleep schedule because I had to catch the 4.15 a.m. bus – the only one with a connection to

Fredericton, New Brunswick, my next stop!

I enjoyed my stay here at Rivière-du-Loup, The hostel was very comfortable, the staff: Guylou, Danny and Jennifer were very friendly, and the two evening excursions were most enjoyable.

Night at Auberge Internationale Rivière-du-Loup.

Day 201 Canada Day. Thursday July 1. Rivière-du-Loup to Fredericton.

Arrived at hostel at 12.30 p.m. and was lucky enough to be able to leave my bags, as check-in time is not until 4 o'clock. I wandered through town ending up by the St. John River where I went to sleep on the grass in the warm sunshine.

This town is the provincial capital of New Brunswick and named after Prince Frederick, second son of King George Ⅲ. The hostel I'm staying in was originally, in 1893, a grammar school, and has since also been the public library. There are only 4 people staying at the hostel, including me, so it's more comfortable than the big city ones, which are too crowded.

Today is Canada Day, and there are great celebrations going on all over Canada to celebrate 125 years since Confederation. I saw the procession here in Fredericton, with floats from all sections of the community, clubs etc., military bands, and Scots Guards. Then there were speeches outside city hall and flag raising, followed by cutting of the cake - two cakes actually. I got in line for my piece of cake, feeling at one with all Canadians, on their day of celebration, and marvelling at the vastness of their country, having travelled 6,500 miles since I entered the Yukon six weeks ago.

Imagine two cakes for the whole city! But then it's only a small city, and there aren't many tourists. It would be nice to have such a cake for Ruislip, my home town, on a day that might be called 'Great Britain Day'. I took photos for my daughter Claire, who is adept at cakemaking, to give her ideas on such cakes!

At 10 o'clock I watched the fireworks display over the

river from outside the hostel. The weather was fine all day.

Night at the York House Hostel, Fredericton.

Day 202. Friday July 2. Fredericton.

This hostel provides breakfast for $3, dinner for $5, both of which must be ordered and paid for in advance, so I ordered both meals for today as it would save me having to search around for somewhere to eat! Breakfast is at 7.30–8.30, which I interpreted as meaning that at any time between this one hour period you could get breakfast, so I arrived in the dining room at 7.55, but it wasn't ready until 8.30. There was a similar wait for dinner, and I never found out the reason for the delay – there were only four people to cook for! I shall breakfast out tomorrow.

I went to the Beaverbrook Art Gallery today, just happened to walk in when the preview of a new exhibition was about to start – Modern Art, needless to say – so there was no charge because it was preview day. Also free coffee and biscuits afterwards.

The reader will be aware of my observations on the Modern Art I saw in Ottawa last week. Well! This artistic creation was different from any other outrageous art that I've seen. It was electro-mechanical. It worked like a child's toy, only it was on a bigger scale. There were three 'creations', but the main one was called *Ecotopia – The Season of Return*, and its theme was of migrating birds. Imagine the metal struts, bars, and beams necessary to transport a small cable car from one side of a large room to the other side, but instead of a cable car there was a wooden platform 4ft x 3ft, on which were 10 toy like wooden birds with wings that were hinged so they could flap. When the electric motor is switched on, the platform travels slowly to the other end 40ft away (it's a large room), with all the wings flapping. It then turns through 180 degrees and returns slowly to the beginning. This cycle repeats continuously for about 15 minutes. Throughout there are musical sound effects of the sea, waves, storms etc. that the birds might encounter on their migratory flight.

After 10 minutes I was bored and thought it might go on forever, so I went to the adjacent lobby for the coffee and snacks, and studied the wall-sized *Santiago El Grande* by Salvador Dali.

Ecotopia was ingenious, an electro-mechanical novelty, and must have taken hundreds of hours to construct, but was it art...? Not in my estimation! Novelty art – yes! or experimental art. Trying to push the boundaries of art to the limit so that it becomes difficult to see it as art. Yet it was exhibited in the prestigious Beaverbrook Art Gallery. I think it's time to close this journal for today!

Night at York House Hostel, Fredericton.

Day 203 Saturday July 3. Fredericton to Charlottetown

I meant to get up at early at 7 a.m. to walk over the bridge to the other side of the river, but overslept till 8.40, so only had time to check out at 9.30. just as the hostel was closing for the day. I had breakfast in a restaurant on the way to the bus depot, left my luggage in a locker and had one hour to spare, so I walked on the riverfront.

The bus departed at 12 noon arriving Moncton 2.45, then a 3 hour stop over before 5.45 p.m. bus to Charlottetown, capital town of Prince Edward Island.

I had a fruit lunch in Moncton, then went to explore a natural phenomenon called a Tidal Bore, which occurs twice daily on the Petitcodiac River at Tidal Bore Park in Moncton. Today's tides were 10 a.m. and 10.30 p.m. so I was unable to see it. I investigated further in the local museum, and visited a viewing point by the river where a platform and floodlights are set up. I will explain the detail if I see it on my return from P.E.I. (Prince Edward Island).

The bus went straight on to the ferry which was a 45 minute crossing, and arrived Charlottetown 10 p.m. I took a taxi to the hostel as it was 3 kilometres out of town. There are only four other people staying here, and I have a dormitory to myself.

Night at Charlottetown International Hostel. P.E.I.

Day 204. Sunday July 4. Charlottetown.

There was a big thunderstorm in the night, and this hostel, which is a restored barn, now leaks in many places. It rained all morning, only a drizzle, so it could have been worse. I walked the 3 kilometres to town – it's still warm and very humid, tiring weather. Shops are closed today, Sunday, and there is nothing much to do, so I went on a city tour, a bus tour, on an old traditional London Bus, which the bus company has owned since 1972.

Then I went on a guided tour of Province House, the P.E.I. parliament building which is restored, but still used for parliamentary sittings. The building is maintained in the same style as it was in 1864, when a meeting took place of ministers (who are now known as The Confederation Fathers) from the two maritime provinces – Nova Scotia and New Brunswick – and Upper Canada (Toronto) and Lower Canada (Quebec). This historic meeting is recognized as being where the foundations were laid for the future confederation which was eventually approved by the Queen in 1867, when Canada was born! Prince Edward Island itself did not become a member province until some years later.

I visited a gallery of modern art, mainly abstract paintings and sculptures, then walked along the harbour front in the warm afternoon sun. I walked the long way back to the hostel in order to buy some food for my evening meal. On the way I met another hosteller, a German girl whom I had met only a few days ago at Rivière–du–Loup. She had just arrived at the hostel and was taking an early evening stroll...

I keep on meeting people who are hostellers travelling much the same route as me. There are usually hostels in places that are interesting to travellers, and here in the maritime provinces there aren't many hostels, so it's quite likely that I'll meet someone more than once. She had been on the Aster Observatory excursion from Rivière–du–Loup.

It is now late evening and I can't decide whether or not to leave here tomorrow. The bus and ferry schedules for travelling from P.E.I. to Newfoundland are complicated. I must leave on the 7.45 a.m. bus to get connections to

Sydney in time to catch the overnight ferry to Newfoundland. There is only one other bus, which leaves here at 12.30 p.m. but this means I would have to stop over somewhere on route to Sydney, which I'm not keen on doing...so in the event of my indecision I am staying a further day and leave on the early bus Tuesday to arrive St. John's Newfoundland about 9 p.m. Wednesday...a long journey of 37 hours...! Bus–ferry–bus–bus–ferry–bus.

Night at Charlottetown International Hostel, P.E.I.

Day 205. Monday July 5. Prince Edward Island.

Another cold, windy and wet morning – I wished I'd caught this morning's early bus to get away from this island which is much bigger than I had thought – 144 miles long by 44 miles wide, and no local buses, only an expensive tour bus to the north which visits the house of 'Green Gables', the setting for the novel 'Anne of Green Gables', the famous book by Lucy Montgomery.

I had no clear idea what I was going to do today, so I walked in the rain to the downtown area – at least the shops were open it being Monday. I went to see a pharmacist to buy got some anti–histamine cream for an itching and watering eye.

Fortune favoured me this morning because I again met the German girl from the hostel, whom I had met yesterday. Her name is Ina, she speaks pretty good French and English, and teaches handicapped children in Hannover. She also didn't know what to do for the day! So we ended up sharing the cost of a hire car, which is the only way of seeing the island.

Rental arrangements completed, we set off at 12 noon, and by mid–afternoon the weather had changed to clear skies, sun and no wind. We followed a prepared route called The Blue Heron Trail, and did in fact see many Blue Heron. Also visited the previously mentioned house of 'Green Gables'. which is actually a museum depicting the period setting of the novel by Lucy Montgomery, who was born, and spent her childhood, on P.E.I.

It is very pleasant driving on P.E.I. as along the

roadsides and hedgerows there is an abundance of wild lupins.

Night at Charlottetown International Hostel, P.E.I.

Day 206 Tuesday July 6. P.E.I. to Sydney Nova Scotia

Ina gave me a lift to the bus station in our hire car, as the hire period is until 12 noon today, and she is staying on P.E.I. another day. There is another hosteller catching my early morning bus, a young lady from Wales who is on vacation from her job as a Nanny to a family near Toronto.

2.30 p.m. Today is a pleasant sunny day and I'm in Truro Bus Depot waiting for the Sydney bus, having already been on a bus, a ferry, and another bus to get here. During the day I have occasionally chatted to the above mentioned young lady from Wales called Nicola, who is staying in Truro a few days. She will be looking for a job in London as a nanny, when her present contract expires in November, so I promised to put her in touch with my daughter Jill if she would contact me nearer the time, as Jill employs a Nanny and may know other families wanting a Nanny. Nicola's camera went wrong during her stay on P.E.I. so I promised to send her a few copies of my photos, which she insisted on paying for on the spot.

The ferry crossing from P.E.I. was calm and clear, but I saw no whales. On the ferry I met Anne of Green Gables! She was dressed like Anne as in the book, from head to toe. She is one of many Annes who mingle with the tourists on the ferries, and everyone wants to take her photograph with ginger hair in ponytail, straw bonnet, and green outfit, and looking very appealing! She is very good for tourism! All the Annes are employed by the government for the summer season and must be high school or university girls, the clothes going with the job, as does the ginger wig if necessary! There are many other summer jobs given to students, from gardening to helping in government laboratories, but to be selected for the job of 'Anne' is an honour for any girl. All this was told to me by the bus driver who has twin girls doing other government summer jobs.

Yesterday in Charlottetown, in Province House, there were two episodes of mini-theatre depicting life as it was around the house at the time of that important meeting in 1864. One episode was by the housekeeper telling us about the extra work entailed in looking after the needs of the ministers at the meeting. The other was four men and a woman (one of the wives) talking on the steps of the building after a meeting had ended, just like M.P.'s might talk freely and casually after a sitting of the House of Commons in England. It was very entertaining!

Today I've been travelling through Nova Scotia for most of the day. It's lovely, green and wooded.

Night on Ferry to Newfoundland.

Day 207. Wednesday July 7. Port aux Basques To Woody Point.

Arrived at North Sydney ferry terminal 9 p.m. last night, the ferry should have sailed at 1.30 a.m. but was late so sailed at 4 a.m. There is normally a connection with the bus in Newfoundland, the ferry normally arriving at 7 a.m., the bus departing at 8 a.m., but as the ferry was 2½ hours late the bus did not wait. The next bus was the following day! So it looked like I was going to waste a day. However, five angry passengers, including me, got together and complained to the ferry company manager. Eventually taxis were laid on at normal bus fare prices, to replace the missed bus, but only to Deer Lake, which happened to be where I was going. The others would have to make their own way after that.

I had five hours to wait before my scheduled bus connection to Woody Point at 5.30 p.m. so I had lunch with the other people from my bus who were all in a bad mood because of the late ferry and missed bus, also one lady had lost her luggage. They were trying to arrange for friends to pick them up rather than use taxis. I then walked around the nearby roads for a couple of hours in the hot sun, but there wasn't much to see and the town was too far to walk to...it was strange to have the bus depot so far out of town, a small office in a gas service station.

I arrived at the Woody Point hostel at 6.30 p.m.– and let myself in – there was a note inside "Make yourself at home, I'll see you later, Emma Gillam." She came in later to collect my money. This hostel is very basic, and only one other person staying, a Swiss fellow.

All the hostels are crammed full of notices, usually bits of paper stuck on walls, informing what you must do, or must not do, or just information. Some examples, chosen from various hostels:

For Sale, Fresh Cod and Caplins.
Check-in 4 p.m. to 11 p.m. Check-out 11 a.m.
Doors Locked 11 p.m.
Quiet Time 11 p.m.
Take Your Shoes Off – Leave in Hall.
No Bare Feet. (A different hostel from above notice)
Don't Put Paper Towels in Toilet.
Wash and Put Away Your Own Dishes.
$2 A Night Sheet Hire.

This last is what I normally have to do, and usually get a towel thrown in free as I don't carry one with me, but not at this hostel, as they haven't anything like that here, so I go without sheet and towel – dry myself with toilet paper after a shower!

The manager girl Emma doesn't live in, she lives in the village.

Night at Woody Point Hostel, Bonne Bay Newfoundland

Day 208. Thursday July 8. Newfoundland.

The bus driver from Deer Lake yesterday told me I ought to go to Trout River Pond – there is no bus, but hitch hiking the 20 kilometres would be no problem. This morning at 11.30 I duly set off and started walking along the road to Trout River Pond, but after one hour and about 2 kilometres I gave up as no one stopped for me. Maybe I wasn't pretty enough! I came back to the village and had a snack in a coffee shop attached to the Stornoway Lodge Motel. It was my lucky day! I had chatted to the waitress about my unsuccessful attempt at hitch hiking, and she later came in to tell me that there were two guests of the motel who were just about to set off for Trout River Pond in a car and would be pleased to give me a lift, there and back. That was nice of the waitress! She went out of her way to help me get a lift. The couple were American, in a big American car.

Trout River Pond is about 20 kilometres long, and quite narrow, but is really two lakes, or fjords, a big and a small, connected by a narrow strip of shallow water, and surrounded by an area called Tablelands. We went on a boat trip round this 'pond'.

This area is a geological phenomenon which at first mystified scientists, but later provided solid evidence for the theory of drifting continents.

500 million years ago there was a continental collision (drift) between Europe and North America which uplifted strata of rock up to 15 kilometres deep and turned them onto the surface.

One side of this 'Pond' is from rock strata of granite type (Peridotite) from 15 kilometres deep, and is now sheer vertical cliff 500 metres high – dark and sombre! The other side is from rock strata of a softer type (Gabbro) from 11 kilometres deep which has eroded and is now gently sloping red rock from water level to a long way back at 650 metres high – a more pleasing landscape!

So the two sides of The Pond are very contrasting and unusual as viewed from a boat gliding its way from one end to the other, and back again.

The American couple I went with were from Louisville, Kentucky, and their car was a Lincoln Town Car, which I rather liked, and wouldn't mind owning!

When I arrived back at the hostel there was another hosteller just arrived today. He's Chinese, but living in Canada. He told me what happened to him in China at the time of the Cultural Revolution in the sixties. The government stopped his education – he was just about to go to university – and sent him to Mongolia to work on farms, with no further education. He was forced to do this for 19 years. The Swiss man has now left the hostel.

The hostel here is like an old fashioned scouts or brownies hall, or community hall, with a stage at one end. There is a built in open plan kitchen at the other end; in the middle are chairs and tables for about 12 people, and 12 beds near the stage with a small room divider separating six of them from the other six, presumably a token attempt to separate the sexes, But it's really just one big hall.

Night at Woody Point Hostel, Bonne Bay Newfoundland

Day 209. Friday July 9. Woody Point to Port aux Basques.

Woody Point is a tiny village with a grocery store, a few handicraft shops, a motel with restaurant, two small churches which are both locked, a cafeteria, and a few rows of houses. All the buildings are wood, it's all very quaint, and on ground sloping down to the water's edge.

It's on an inlet arm off Bonne Bay, and across the water (maybe 2 kilometres, although it's likely to be more), are two larger towns which are nearer the interesting parts of the Gros Morne National Park, in which all this area lies...but I can't get to it from here! There was a ferry across the inlet arm to Norris Point, but it stopped running last summer. The only way is by road, about 60 kilometres, and there is no bus service, so the only way to get there is by renting a car. The nearest rent-a-car is on the main Canada Highway at Deer Lake, 70 kilometres away and served by the one bus a day that I was on yesterday.

I considered hiring a car and staying a couple more days to make it worthwhile, but decided against it. The distances involved between places of interest are so great that I'd be driving all day, and there's no one to share a car with – it's not much fun on your own anyway! Newfoundland is vast, bigger than I thought. So apart from what I did yesterday at Trout River Pond, there's nothing else to do here at Woody Point.

It's a quiet and sleepy place, but not hot enough to lie in the sun by the water's edge – there are no foot trails alongside the water, and the road ends a little further past Woody Point. It's a good place for sketching the wooden houses and churches.

Away from the road there are vast tracts of bush land, and fir, pine and spruce trees. The island is full of moose and caribou, so people say, and the men have hunting and firearm licences to kill game. They supplement their meagre income by using the animals for food and selling the remains to animal processors. It is all strictly controlled; each kill has to be reported to game wardens, and only a limited number are allowed over the whole island each season, then it is stopped until the next season. But I haven't seen any of this wildlife! There is also bear here, but again not seen by me.

So I've decided that Newfoundland is too big to explore in a few days without a good bus service, and I'm not renting a car because distances are too great driving on my own. I want to explore Nova Scotia a little more during my last week in this part of the world, Halifax being my point of departure.

I left a message for the bus driver at the gas station in Woody Point: "Pick up Mr. Bonney at the International Hostel in the morning." Such is the personal service you get from people in this sleepy little village. He had told me to leave such a message when he dropped me here two days ago, when I knew the day I was leaving. He has to go to the gas station each morning to fill up with gas, so he will get the message, which was written on the office memo pad.

He also picks up and delivers parcels and computer print-outs from and to various shops. He delivered a mail order package to a lady who actually boarded the bus, and she immediately opened her parcel of new shoes in front of everyone before even thinking of paying her fare! You don't get people getting on the bus with their chickens and goats as in India and Bali and such places, but the driver had to drive to the bank at Deer Lake for one lady passenger who decided she had to get some money out – "I hope no one minds," she said, looking at me, as I was the only apparent stranger who might! I said I didn't mind as I had plenty of time. To the driver, it seemed to be all in a day's work. We waited 10 minutes in the bank car park.

The above scenario is what Newfoundland is like. A lady

I met somewhere on mainland Canada said they tell jokes about Newfoundlanders because they are so slow and laid back, but I found them really friendly and helpful...In the grocery store this morning I was offered coffee, which was very welcome as I don't have it in the hostel. It was free! I only bought a bar of chocolate, and then hurried back to the hostel to be ready for the bus at 9.30 a.m. It was on time..! The driver did get my message.

We arrived at Corner Brook, my destination, half an hour later than the scheduled time, but I still had 7 hours stopover before my bus connection for Port aux Basques at 6.30 p.m.

Corner Brook is the second largest town next to St. John's. I walked the 3 kilometres to downtown, and a further 2 km. out the other side to the Captain Cook Memorial on a hill overlooking the town and the Bay of Islands, and further out, the Gulf of St. Lawrence. I spent a relaxing hour here appreciating the view and eating lunch.

I could have stayed overnight here at Corner Brook – it is quite a pleasant town – but I would also have to stay until tomorrow evening as there is only the one bus a day to Port aux Basques for the ferry. The problem is that on a Friday the bus doesn't get there in time to catch the night ferry at 8 p.m. – the bus arrives 9.15 p.m. On other days the ferry departs 11.30 p.m. I decided to go to Port aux Basques today and spend the night in the ferry terminal, so I can then catch the morning ferry at 9 a.m.

On arriving at Port aux Basques I found my way out of the large dock area just as it was getting dark, and walked until I found a restaurant in the town area. I didn't relish the thought of coming back in the dark! However, nothing untoward happened.

Overnight in Ferry Terminal, Port aux Basques.

Day 210. Saturday July 10. Port aux Basques to Sydney.

I spent an uncomfortable night in the ferry terminal waiting room, and quite a pleasant 5 hour crossing on this huge ferry M.V. Caribou, like a cruise ship – it holds 1200 passengers and 350 cars. Arrived North Sydney 2 p.m. and caught a local transit bus to downtown Sydney, 22 kilometres away. From the bus window I spotted a hotel on the harbour front that I had seen in the Lonely Planet Guide – Paul's Hotel. I walked back from the bus station and checked in for $32, in a room overlooking Sydney harbour. The reader should note that this is not to be confused with the grandeur of the other Sydney harbour in Australia – this is just a small town in Nova Scotia!

I later walked around the town and did mundane things like posting a parcel home, containing travel brochures.

Night at Paul's Hotel, Sydney, Nova Scotia.

Day 211. Sunday July 11. Sydney.

I intended to have an easy day..! Maybe lazing in the sun by the harbour front...but at breakfast the manager lady suggested I went to the only place worth seeing around here, called Fort Louisbourg. As it wasn't sunny and warm, I couldn't laze around the harbour, so I decided to go. It meant hitch-hiking as there was no public transport. She, the landlady, gave me a lift to a strategic point for hitch-hiking, on her way to church. It's 22 kilometres to Louisbourg.

I don't know why I do such things! Drivers just don't stop for me. Maybe I look too much of a wreck, after travelling the world for so long! Anyway, I think I'm too old for this sort of thing, especially after my failed attempt at hitch-hiking in Newfoundland! I got a lift after 50 minutes. Coming back I had to wait 1 hour 50 minutes...I was beginning to think I would have to stay the night!

Louisbourg is a reconstructed walled city as at 1744, before it was attacked by the British in 1758. The British won that battle and the French fled. It is a living reconstruction with many soldiers and women and children dressed as in that period. The French soldiers on guard at the gates challenged everyone on entry, and gave me, in particular, a hard time (in mock), as they thought I was British. I said I was Australian as a lot of people on my travels have thought I was, but they wouldn't accept that, saying that if you're Australian, you're still British! I countered by saying that I had been told there was a special truce today as a Walt Disney film is being made on the site! Anyway, it was all in good fun.

The film will be called 'Squanto', and is set in the early 1600's, to be released in the spring of 1994. I saw quite a few scenes being shot, so I will make a point of seeing it on release. It added another interest to the visit, and because of inconvenience to visitors, Walt Disney Productions paid half the entrance fees. The whole place was cold and damp, as a mist lay over the sea, and visibility was poor, but I was prepared for the cold, and it made the place more realistic as, according to the brochure, it was noted for this sort of weather all those centuries ago.

When I finally returned to Sydney, after my long wait for a lift, it was 5.30 p.m. and the sun was shining, so I sat by the harbour for an hour. Later, I had an excellent Chinese meal: Chow Mein, Chicken Fried Rice, Sweet and Sour Pork Balls, and Egg Roll. Yesterday I also had a good meal of Honey Glazed Pork Chops, Baked Jacket Potato, and Vegetables. I haven't had proper meals for a long time, what with cooking for myself at hostels, and meals on bus journeys and ferries.

Night at Paul's Hotel, Sydney, Nova Scotia.

Day 212. Monday July 12. Sydney to Truro.

I'm on the 11 a.m. bus from Sydney to Truro. Sydney is on Cape Breton Island and only connected to mainland Nova Scotia by the bridge at Port Hastings. It's quite a big island – about 150 x 120 kilometres – and in days gone by was of strategic military importance, with the fortress of Louisbourg on the south east corner guarding against invaders. The island has so much water within it, rivers, lakes large and small, inlets and bays, that the scenery is constantly changing and very impressive. On the bus we pass mile after mile of fir, spruce and pine trees; there is a Highlands National Park, but I won't see it as it is in the north, and my route is east to west, to Port Hastings.

The place names here in Nova Scotia are very confusing to the mind. During a lifetime one associates a name with a place: I've just left Sydney and my mind tells me it is in Australia – it left an impression on me when I was there in April with Pat for 10 days. I'm on the bus going to Truro, which of course, my mind tells me, is in Cornwall! I really do forget sometimes which country I'm in. Just travelling, in itself, through so many countries, is sometimes disorientating – you have to think hard to get your mind up to date as to where you are at this moment, and where you are going...am I still in Newfoundland..? or Prince Edward Island..? Where was I two days ago..? When I miss writing this journal for a day or two, I have to think hard about what I did, and where I was...

1.30 p.m. There has been fog (mist, I suppose, as there is no pollution here) all the morning, and it has now turned to rain. We had a lot of rain in Sydney last night, I just managed to run back from the Chinese restaurant before it came down heavily.

Back to place names.....Yet, a few months back, in Indonesia when I was 7 or 8 days behind, I had no trouble in remembering. I guess that the brain, wonderful piece of memory equipment that it is, has a saturation point, and my brain is finding it difficult to store recent event data, as there are too many recent events! It is fortunate that I keep a journal! In Nova Scotia alone there are Sydney, Truro, Halifax, Dartmouth, Windsor, Yarmouth, just to name the larger places with the same names as English towns. Then the smaller towns are Brighton, Oxford, Liverpool, Bridgewater, Berwick, Bedford, New Glasgow and New Edinburgh ('New' because Nova Scotia means New Scotland). It is strange having all these familiar place names in a different country!

Canada is so vast! And the provinces so different! People who I meet talk about their provinces as if they are a separate country. The climate and culture is so different, for example, in the Yukon, compared to 6,000 miles away in Newfoundland. Then there is Quebec with its so different French culture! In a restaurant in Sydney, a waiter asked me what it was like in the Yukon – he had no idea! He said he was never likely to go to such a far away place!

Regarding laws and issues concerning the whole of Canada, there is a Federal government which controls all these things. There is one issue that people in all provinces seem to be united on, and that is that Canada does not become part of the United States of America. There seems to be some political pressure for this to happen, but people generally do not want it, they are proud of their Canada.

As a point of interest I have visited all ten provinces and the two territories.

Night at the Willow Bend Motel, Truro.

Day 213. Tuesday July 13. Truro.

I'm having 4 days of comparative luxury as I stayed 2 days in a Sydney hotel, and now 2 days in this motel in Truro, with breakfast included in both places, and also towels and soap provided. I don't carry a towel, but normally hire one in hostels for a dollar, except if they don't have any, in which case I go without.

Today I walked round downtown Truro, shopping, and visited Victoria Park, which is enormous, and very pleasant. I would have liked to stay longer, but had to get to the River Salmon in time to see a Tidal Bore...

Yesterday evening I walked four kilometres to the River Salmon to see a Tidal Bore (which I reported upon in Moncton – day 203). I arrived at the scheduled time of 7.21 p.m. but I missed it, or it never came! I don't know which, because no one else present by the river side knew the reason, they being tourists like me. So this evening I went again, and thinking I would make sure this time by getting there 18 minutes early – surely a tide couldn't be that much early? But it was! Someone told me it had arrived two minutes ago. So I'll have to go again early tomorrow morning, the Tidal Bore scheduled time being at 8.47 a.m.

I had dinner in Wendy's, which is a little upmarket from McDonald's. This I had planned after the Tidal Bore visit, then walked back the 4 kilometres to the motel. On reflection, I should have stayed near the River Salmon, as there are budget motels nearby, thereby avoiding all this walking back and forth...but it keeps me fit! The motel where I'm staying has a swimming pool, and has the great advantage of being opposite the bus depot, thus I don't have far to carry my bags.

Night at Willow Bend Motel, Truro.

Day 214. Wednesday July 14. Truro to Halifax.

I decided in the end to go by taxi, so as to get to the river early, not wanting to miss this tidal bore a third time! I arrived 40 minutes early, and actually saw it!

Tidal Bore. The tides in the Bay of Fundy are the highest in the world. The explanation for these tides is in the length, depth, and gradual funnel shape of the bay. As the high tide builds up, the water flowing into the narrowing bay has to rise on the edges. It is pushed still higher by the shallowing sea bed. A compounding factor is called resonance...this refers to the sloshing or rocking back and forth from one end to the other of all the water in the bay, like a giant bath tub. When this mass swell is on the way out of the bay and meets a more powerful incoming tide head on, the volume of water increases substantially. The difference between low and high tide in this bay is between 10 and 15 metres, and has been 16.6 metres (54ft). Another place where there are noteworthy high tides is in Bristol, England. When this advancing tide reaches the feeding rivers it pushes up river, reversing the normal flow of the river, thereby causing a wave, called a Tidal Bore, which can vary in height up to a metre. The one I saw this morning was on the River Salmon at Truro, but it was only about 6 inches high. All these effects are at their most extreme when the moon and the sun are in line with the earth.

After the morning's excitement of Tidal Bore watching I relaxed by and in the swimming pool. I very nearly missed the 6 inch high Tidal Bore because I didn't know what to expect, until someone shouted, "Is that it?" after it had gone past me, so I had to chase after it to get photos!

I caught the 1.30 p.m. bus to Halifax, and arrived at the hostel at 4 p.m. Walked around the waterfront area and eventually had a spaghetti bolognaise 'eat as much as you like' meal. I'm in a room for two with shower and facilities. My room mate is a hostel manager from Banff who is touring the maritime area looking for possible sites for new hostels.

Night at Halifax Heritage House Hostel.

Day 215. Thursday July 15. Halifax.

I spent the whole day shopping!

Security of Baggage. During my trip I have developed a system for keeping my valuables reasonably secure from loss or theft, having met many people, and heard of others, who have lost, or had stolen, luggage, wallets, cameras etc. while travelling.

I was reminded of all this when I got off the Newfoundland ferry at Port-aux-Basques from Sydney, when, on collecting our checked in luggage, one lady waited, and waited, for hers to appear, but it never did. Eventually, the baggage handler made a phone call to Sydney where a search was started. Later the Sydney police phoned to say they had found her luggage bag on the grass behind the ferry terminal, with locks forced open and contents spread on the grass. The thief had taken only her cheque book and credit card, leaving all clothes etc. as obviously worthless! Fancy putting cheque book and credit card with your checked in luggage! My checked in bag was in the same truck as hers, and might well have been stolen, but it contained only clothes, and would not have made much difference to my holiday. This lady was in the same group as me which missed the connecting bus at Port-aux-Basques because the ferry was late arriving. I had lunch at Deer Lake with three people including this lady...she was very upset and still in a state of shock, and could only keep on saying how she couldn't understand that someone could take her luggage! It was now 5 hours since she was told about her loss, and she hadn't yet told her bank! I told her she must do it immediately, so she went out to make the phone call, but the bank would not put a 'stop' on her account from just a phone call, she must appear in person at the bank. So she had to wait for her friend to pick her up, who arrived shortly afterwards...it was now 16 hours since her luggage was stolen! I never heard what happened as we went our separate ways.

Anyway, about my own security system – you can't carry all your valuables and luggage around with you all the time while travelling, so it's a question of having degrees of security:

Top security is for cash, travellers' cheques, credit card, airline tickets, and passport. These I keep in a neck band wallet, and a few days spending money in a pocket wallet, both wallets always on me, or under my pillow at night.

The next level of security is for my camera, and diary containing information like addresses, details of photos as I take them, and mileage information, also this journal as I write it – these I keep in a hand/shoulder bag – I would be very unhappy if I lost this bag, so I carry it around everywhere, although I do tend to leave it in hostels and motel rooms in the evening when I go out for a meal...I put it inside my large bag which is then padlocked. In the Middle East and Asia I carried it around in the evening as well, never happy with leaving valuables in hotel rooms in those countries. In Pakistan, I did once leave 30 dollars in a coat in a room while at dinner, and it was stolen. I write this journal in duplicate and post the original home every two weeks, keeping the copy in my large bag, so minimizing the risk of losing both copies of any part of it!

Next level of security is my rucksac where I keep my short wave radio, film (exposed and unexposed reels), medicines, copies of important documents (originals are in my body wallet), and a few other things – I should hate to lose these things, but If I did lose my rucksac it wouldn't ruin my trip! I always send each roll of exposed film back to England for processing as soon as possible after taking it out of the camera. This rucksac I never check in as luggage with bus, airline or ferry trips – I keep it with me all the time I'm travelling, as hand luggage.

Next, and lowest level of security is my large luggage bag, which is mainly clothes, books, travel brochures, and many odds and ends. This bag I check in on bus, train, airline, and ferry trips, and hope for the best...hope it doesn't get stolen or lost! I have lost it once in Alaska when the railroad staff didn't take it off the train at Denali, and it went on to Fairbanks. The Alaska Railroad staff were extremely apologetic and sent a pick-up truck to bring it back the following morning. I had spare clothes in my rucksac, so it was no hardship.

These levels of security evolved only gradually over the first weeks of travel. Travelling on trains is a problem, because most of the time we didn't check in baggage – it would have been folly to do it in Egypt and Asia! We just carried it with us on the train, and if you have to stack it at the end of the carriage it's difficult to keep an eye on it. If you're in the buffet car when the train stops at a station, your luggage is at risk because you can't get back to your seat – you can't walk along the corridor because of people getting on and off, so you have to make a point of not being away from your seat when the train is at a station. Intending thieves could walk on with the crowd, and walk off with your case!

I seem to be getting a little careless now, merely because nothing has happened to my luggage or valuables since I had those dollars stolen in Pakistan, which is now six months ago...I intended to leave my luggage in a locker at Sydney bus station because I had an hour to spare, but all the lockers were used; the ticket office clerk said he would keep my case and rucksac behind the counter for the hour, which I accepted – and I didn't even bother to padlock the rucksac!! I guess any security system gets progressively slacker the longer the period since there was a breach in that security. When the security is breached, slackness is tightened up, all possible loop holes are closed...and from then on it gradually gets slacker again...

Thursday evening. Had dinner in the same waterfront restaurant as last night, but this time had pizza for a change plus my now normal glass of beer.

Night at Halifax Heritage House Hostel.

Day 216. Friday July 16. Halifax.

I'm not bothering to cook breakfast in the hostel as it only costs $2.20 in a restaurant.

Went to the Maritime Museum and saw all about the tremendous explosion in Halifax harbour in 1917 when a munitions ship exploded. The ship, the *Mont Blanc*, had collided with another ship causing a fire to break out. The crew abandoned ship, expecting it to blow up immediately, but it burned for twenty minutes, and drifted against a pier in a busy district of the town. The spectacle of the burning ship drew crowds of spectators, and they stood enthralled at what they thought was a safe distance...

The explosion was colossal..! it completely destroyed a large part of the town including 1,630 homes, and killed 1,700 people! There was hardly a pane of glass left intact in Halifax or Dartmouth, which is 1½ kilometres across the water. It was the biggest man made explosion in history until the atomic age. During the planning stage for the bombing of Hiroshima and Nagasaki, the effects of the Halifax explosion were studied, in order to calculate the strength of bombs needed.

There is also a section in the museum on the sinking of the Titanic, as Halifax was the nearest port where rescue operations were mounted, and survivors were taken.

I caught a ferry across the harbour to Dartmouth and went shopping in a large mall, then sat in the sun for an hour by the waterfront taking in the views of the harbour across to Halifax...and trying to imagine what it must have been like on that fateful day, the 6th of December 1917, when that munition ship blew up!

There is a good view of the Citadel, a historic building on a hill in Halifax, which I haven't bothered to visit...my enthusiasm waning somewhat after having seen so many similar buildings around the world in the past 7 months. I returned by ferry, and had dinner in the Cafe Mediterraneo, which is, I discovered during the meal, Lebanese. I had Clam Strips deep fried and French Fries. Clam is a bit chewy like octopus, and of no particular flavour.

I have met an Australian from Canberra who has just cycled from Vancouver in the last two months. His name is Brian Mckay and he's 64 years old – no mean feat! It's 7,000 kilometres from Vancouver, and he's carried a tent, and camped most of the time.

The hostel here at Halifax is very good, with friendly staff. I have been in two different rooms for two and four people respectively, both with toilet, and shower or bath. Not bad for $12.75 per night, and situated quite close to downtown.

Night at Halifax Heritage Hostel.

Day 217. Saturday July 17. Halifax.

It seems like I've been writing this journal for ever! Yesterday evening I fancied a drink so went into a Pub–like establishment, of which Halifax has many. A disc jockey was just starting a Karaoke session, so I prepared myself to walk out at short notice, not liking the idea much – I would probably be bored. As it turned out, it was far from boring!

The D.J. girl sang a few songs, then announced that Fluffy was going to sing. I wondered what someone with a name like that could look like, or whether it was male or female! It turned out he was sitting near me – I hadn't noticed him as the light was dimmed. He was big, with fluffy ginger hair, fluffy beard and sideboards, and wore shorts. He really looked a 'joke'! He didn't look dressed for singing on the stage. He was, so he told me later, a stand up comic, but there wasn't much demand for comics these days.

He sang well, and during the 1½ hours I was there, sang six songs. He told me he has a repertoire of 119. Some other people sang, and I was enjoying myself..! I chatted to Fluffy, whose other name was Karl, and he introduced me to the D.J. girl who was very friendly...they were all so obviously pleased that I was enjoying this, my very first experience of karaoke.

Half way through the evening three blind young men came in with their three guide dogs and sat at my table. One of them was a huge man – about 25 stone. Fluffy introduced me to them, and there was much hand shaking, with very careful finding of hands without knocking over glasses of beer, and being careful not to tread on the dogs who had positioned themselves all round everyone's feet.

The blind guys spoke so loud...the music was playing... someone was singing...the lights were very dim...the bar girl was taking orders for drinks...the drinks came and had to be handed out to the correct hand, which was all very difficult in the near darkness, which didn't affect the blind people, but we sighted ones couldn't see either! There was much conversation, and all the time some person was singing, so no one could hear properly what the other was saying.

The three blind men were a musical 'group', guitar, piano and singer...the singer got up and sang a few songs, and he sang beautifully. They were ecstatic that I, from England, was here talking to them, and listening to their singer...I told them it was a pity I couldn't hear them perform as a group. So a good time was had by all! The blind trio insisted I gave them my address so they could send me their new business card, when it gets printed, so that I will remember them when they get to 'number one'.

This morning I took a trip to Dartmouth (sister town to Halifax), by bus this time, and did shopping at The Bay (Hudson Bay Company), a large department store – slightly upmarket from the normal run of stores here.

After lunch I went on an organized trip to Peggy's Cove, about an hours drive west along the coast from Halifax. It's a quaint little fishing village with a glaciated history. At the end of the last ice age, when the glaciers melted, they left a deposit in and around the Peggy's Cove area, of large isolated granite boulders, called erratics. They look as if they have been planted by a giant hand! 'Peggy' is the name of a lone survivor of a shipwreck a long time ago...so the legend goes.

The Lobster is synonymous with Nova Scotia and Newfoundland, it being one of their major industries, although at the present time it is not the fishing season. However, there is still plenty of fresh lobster available in shops and restaurants, but the meals are expensive...unless you go to McDonald's, the gourmet restaurant, for a McLobster! They have special lobsters with a tartan patterned shell!

Because it is out of the fishing season, lobster traps are stacked up all over wharves and jetties everywhere...and for effect there is one in the lobby of many restaurants, and even one in the hostel on Prince Edward Island. The gift shops are full of model lobster traps of various sizes for tourists.

Stories abound as to how a trap works. The most likely story is that the bait in a trap invites a lobster into the 'kitchen' via a suitable hole, it then eats the bait and explores further forward along a corridor, eventually finding its way into the 'parlour' from which it cannot escape due to its front anatomy, and the way the corridor from the kitchen is designed. Other lobsters see the lobster in the 'parlour' and follow – they are not very intelligent – until the trap is crammed full of lobsters. When the trap is hauled out and opened any lobster less than a certain size is returned to the sea to grow bigger. Our tour guide told us that her mother was put off lobster for life when she was young, because she put a live lobster in boiling water feet first and it screamed in pain! She should have put it in head first so as to kill it instantly.

This evening I dined in McDonald's and had a very enjoyable McLobster with French fries.

Night at Halifax Heritage Hostel.

Days 218–219. Sunday–Monday July 18–19. Halifax to London.

This is the last day of my trip and I can't believe it's over...it's gone on for so long...Egypt seems so long ago, and so much has happened...so many cultural experiences. Looking back over my journey, each stage of the trip seems to be wrapped in a different time capsule, so that they are not connected...not all part of the one continuous round the world trip. I suppose this is because each stage was so different from the previous one – the method of travel so different – and travel companions always different, or I was travelling alone.

This morning I had breakfast with Brian at the Lebanese Cafe, and we later went to the morning service at the United Church, where we were joined by Jim from Auckland, who is a teacher living and teaching in Ontario on a teacher exchange scheme. The church people were delighted to welcome such a representative selection of people from the Commonwealth. We were all invited to coffee and biscuits in the church hall after the service, reminding me of my home town Methodist Church in Eastcote. The lady minister, in her sermon, spoke about God delivering the ten commandments to Moses on Mount Sinai, and also mentioned St. Katherine's Monastery which lies at the foot of the mountain. This was all very relevant to me, having visited the monastery during my stay in the village of St. Katherines in January.

Jim from Auckland spent the next few hours with me strolling along the waterfront, having lunch, and visiting the Halifax Art Gallery, which, as time was pressing, I had to leave in a hurry to get back to the hostel to collect my luggage, and then walk to the nearby Hilton Hotel to catch the 3.50 p.m. airport shuttle bus.

I had to make special arrangements to get into the hostel at 3.15 p.m. which is out of hours, the hostel normally opening at 4 p.m. The receptionist had given me the day's front door lock key code. This key code is normally only available to hostellers after 4 p.m. if they want to stay out later than 10.30 p.m. when the door is locked.

All hostels are different in the time they lock the door at night. Most seem to be 10.30, 11, or midnight, and if you arrive late, then you can't get in! City hostels sometimes have access all night, for example Toronto where there is a receptionist on duty all night, and here at Halifax where the door is locked, but you're allowed to have the door key code. Most hostels close during the daytime, Halifax is between 11 and 4 p.m., while others close for longer periods 9.30 a.m. to 7 p.m. They are all different.

Anyway, when I arrived back at 3.15 p.m. other

hostellers were already in, it was a couple with two children, having their lunch. They were in fact catching the same flight as me to Amsterdam. I caught the shuttle at 3.50 p.m. to the airport – the hostel family was going by taxi, and they needed the whole taxi, no room for me to share. The shuttle cost $11, it's 38 kilometres to the airport, the furthest city airport I've come across on my travels.

I arrived 4.30, flight time 8.30. I had decided to catch an early bus as there was nothing else I wanted to do at this late hour (of my travels), and I had some catching up to do with this journal. As it happens the flight was 2½ hours late in leaving, and surprisingly, the Captain himself came to apologise for the delay three times, finally giving everyone a voucher for free snacks. He told us the fault was in the emergency machinery in the tail section: there was an oil leak and two gaskets needed replacing, which they did not have available in their own stores, but were able to borrow them from Air Canada. The Captain also told us that due to the delay he would take on more fuel and fly faster to catch up some time, a 5½ hour flight instead of the scheduled 6 hours. So we had to cram in drinks, dinner, duty free, a movie, sleep, and breakfast. I didn't sleep much, and couldn't concentrate on the movie. Nevertheless, having caught up half an hour of the 2½ hours delay, we were still 2 hours late at Amsterdam, 9.30 a.m. instead of 7.45 a.m. so I missed my 8.45 a.m. KLM connecting flight to London, and the next one was 1.20 p.m.

All of those who missed connecting flights, and there were many of us, received meal vouchers, so I had a meal and went out of the airport for some air. The passport control and customs didn't like me doing it and questioned me a bit, but finally agreed. It was cold outside...I was worried about my checked in bag...would it get transferred to the correct flight? Did the baggage people know which flight I was catching? I was sitting on a bench seat outside the airport when I suddenly saw my bag being unloaded from a trolley on to a tour bus, so I picked up my rucksac and chased after it, running like mad! But it wasn't my bag...a false alarm. I must be getting edgy!

My new flight was 1.20 p.m. so I went to the departure lounge at 12.30. The flight went smoothly. I didn't know what was happening at 'Heathrow Arrivals', whether Pat and Claire had waited five hours, or gone home, or what.

The new flight arrived on time and they were waiting, having gone home and come back again. KLM had allowed me to send a message home about the new arrival time, but they never received it. It must have been a telephone message and no one answered. They were waiting, Pat and Claire, but they didn't recognize me with my Alaska baseball cap on, and new flowery shirt.

There was a great homecoming, with balloons and flags of all the nations I'd visited, decorating the front porch, and Sarah and Jill and Roseanna and new baby Heather awaiting me!

It's all over! The End!!

Epilogue

I arrived home on Day 219, Monday July 19, but in England it was only the 218th day since I had departed. So I have somehow lived an extra day in my circumnavigation of the globe... The reason is that whilst travelling east across time zones, I was constantly putting the clock forward one hour. So 24 of my days were only 23 hours in length. To make up for these lost 24 hours... on the 30th April when Pat and I crossed the International Date Line in the Pacific Ocean, we put the clock back 24 hours, thereby giving us that extra day, which was also the 30th April. See Days 138 and 139 in diary.

Would I have done anything differently? Yes, I would not have stayed in Paris, Lausanne, and Milan... They were too expensive, and I wasn't in the right mood to enjoy these large cities, having just started on my trip, and still feeling a bit apprehensive – They were lonely and unfriendly! I should have stayed in smaller towns on my way down to Bari to catch the ferry to Egypt.

Not having done anything quite so adventurous before, I didn't know that when I returned I would be asked to give many photographic slide shows. These shows made me realize that there were many photos I didn't take that I should have done, of things and places where I was feeling bad, and low in spirit: photos of Alexandria when I was suffering from culture shock; photos of the dentist and his 'Medieval' surgery in India, when I was scared out of my wits as I sank into that chair; photos of that cold and uncomfortable train journey from Amritsar to Delhi. The fact that I didn't take these photos must surely prove that I'm not really a dedicated photographer... for if I had suddenly been confronted by a bear in Canada, or met a charging rhinoceros on my safari in Nepal, I'm sure that the last thing to enter my mind would be to calmly get my camera out and take that photograph to show them back home...! Maybe next time will be different!

Index